The Spirit of COLLIN COUNTY

Featuring Photography by Barry Benton
Narrative by Guy Giersch

A publication of the Collin County Association of REALTORS®

Historical Publishing Network
A division of Lammert, Inc.
San Antonio, Texas

CONTENTS

First Edition

ISBN: 9781893619692
Library of Congress Card Catalog Number: 2007922623

The Spirit of Collin County

photographer: Barry Benton
author: Guy Giersch
contributing writers for "Sharing the Heritage": Eric Dabney, Cyndy Moore

Historical Publishing Network

president: Ron Lammert

project managers: Barbara Lane, Joe Neely, Robin Neely

administration: Donna M. Mata, Evelyn Hart

book sales: Dee Steidle

production: Colin Hart, Charles A. Newton, III, Craig Mitchell

PRINTED IN SOUTH KOREA

Introduction

They came to Collin County in covered wagons, on horseback and even on foot to settle this land ripe with virgin forests, streams, and open prairies. Land-starved people from the heavily settled eastern states saw fresh opportunities in the open land of the northern part of the newly formed Republic of Texas. The allure that brought the early pioneers to Collin County then is still unchanged as new pioneers and entrepreneurs now come in their SUV's, pickup trucks, and mini-vans to settle in this land ripe with real estate investments, business opportunities, and leisurely lifestyle activities. This pioneer spirit that is the American experience thrives in Collin County, making it the 11th fastest growing counties in America – and one of the best places in the country to live.

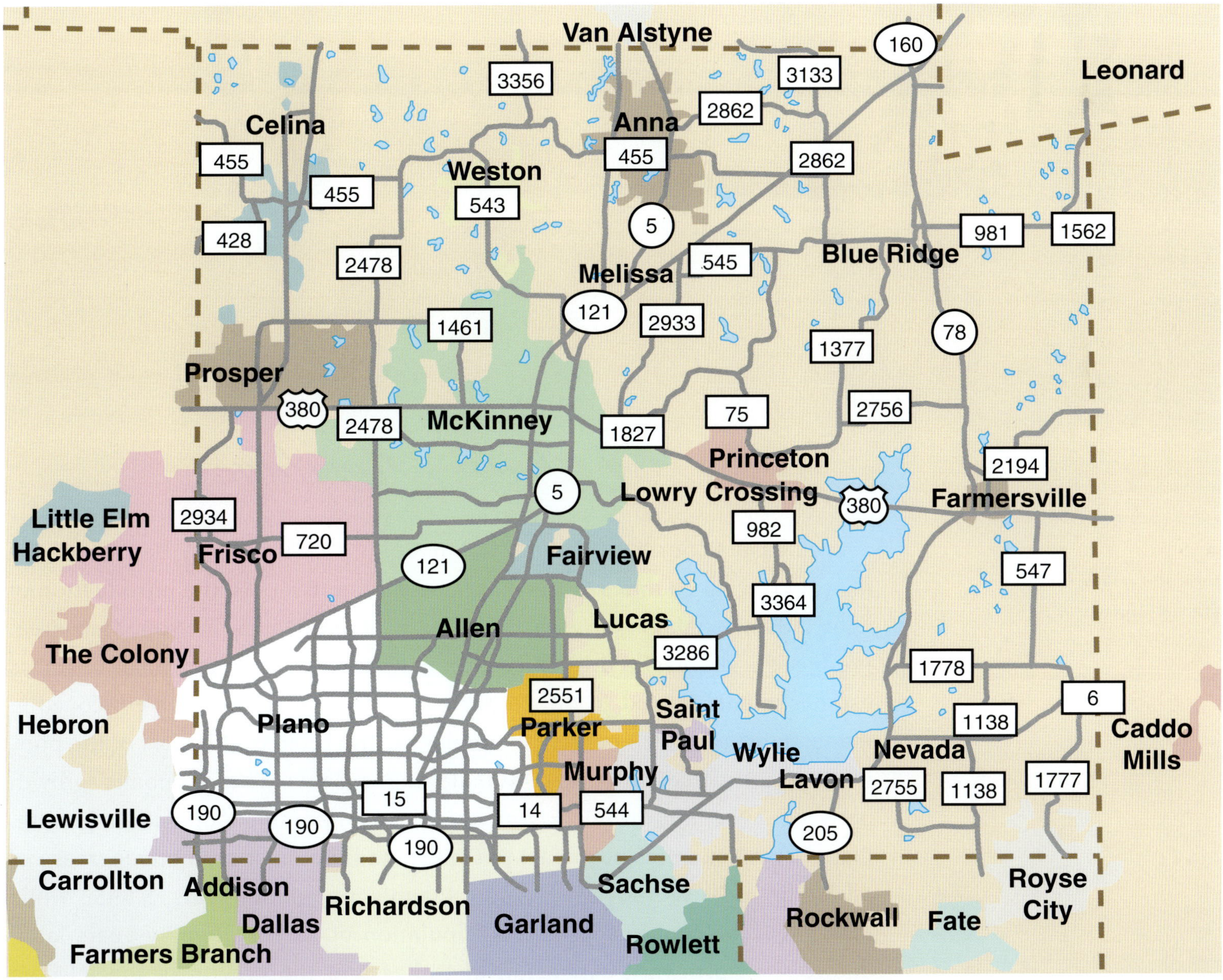

A Rich Heritage

★
Longhorns at Craig Ranch, McKinney, Texas.
PHOTO COURTESY OF GUY GIERSCH

Located just north of Dallas, Collin County continues to be one of the fastest growing counties in the state and nation. By 1980 the introduction of light industry, combined with the growth of the Dallas metropolitan area, produced a successful diversified economy. In 1980 the number of business establishments totaled 2,388; 25 percent of the population was employed in manufacturing and 23 percent in wholesale and retail trade. Most of the population, 59 percent, worked outside the county. The economic growth between 1960 and 1980 accompanied a comparable population growth. Plano, eighteen miles northeast of Dallas, had the most dramatic increase of all Collin County towns: in 1960 Plano's population was 3,695, while McKinney, the county seat had a population of 13,763. Twenty years later, due to the northward expansion of Dallas and the growth of the telecom business, Plano's population soared to 72,331 while other cities in Collin County remained relatively unchanged. Today, Plano's population is 250,096 according to the 2005 census estimate. Overall, Collin County's population increased from 41,692 in 1960 to 144,576 in 1980. Subsequently it continued to grow, largely as a result of the development of the suburbs in and around Plano and Collin County's population as of 2000 census is 491,675 making it 8th largest of the 254 counties in Texas. According to the North Central Texas Council of Governments, the population of Collin County increased at a rate of 5.74% during 2005-2006, which brings the current population of the County to be over 690,000 residents in 2006.

Climate, combined with fertile Blackland Prairie soils allowed for two types of growth. The land provided space to grow a population and land to grow crops. Fertile soils and entrepreneurial drive among the settlers helped make Collin County one of the largest producers of cotton in Texas during the 1920's. In 1926 the county was the sixth largest cotton-producing area in the US. Besides cotton, the land produced a variety of grains such as corn and wheat. These products bolstered the early economy and in response to the

★
Working farms still exist in Collin County.

tremendous agricultural production; gins, flourmills, and one of three textile plants west of the Mississippi that made denim cloth added to the economic well being of the county.

Agriculture eventually lost its dominance as an economic force, but the land is still providing opportunities for a new type of growth and a new type of pioneer. The new pioneers are coming to grow businesses and enjoy a lifestyle that is unique to North Texas. A mild temperature throughout most of the year, provides a growing season that is approximately 237 days long, and sports an average rainfall just under thirty-five inches a year. The climate that helped produce record crops at one time is the same climate which now provides for a high quality lifestyle.

25EEE
Not
For
Sale

A&L

★

Right: Bending iron the old way. What was once a necessity is now an art form.

Opposite: Historic homes abound in Collin County.

★

The home of H.L. Wells, an early settler in Collin County, still stands as a testament to the past.

★
Old Collin County Courthouse was restored in 2006 to become the McKinney Performing Arts Center.

SACHSE
CHAMBER OF
COMMERCE
Sachse
Shines!
SACHSE CHAMBER
OF COMMERCE
972-496-1212
RAIL
ROAD
CROSSING

PARKER COUNTY TEXAS
PEACHES
Sweet
$1.99 LB

★
Interurban Museum in Plano, Texas.

& War
TEXAS
BACKYARD
BBQ
Shiner

McKINNEY

Welcome To
WYLIE
Since 1886

A Great Place to Live

★
Collin County is home to numerous Texas State Championship football teams.

Sports are a major business as well as a participatory activity for Collin County residents. The tremendous opportunities offered in Collin County have prompted individuals like gold medal Olympian Michael Johnson to build his Performance Center to serve local, national, and international athletes near the Cooper Training Clinic and Living Center in Craig Ranch. These facilities bring another dimension to the quality lifestyle already being offered.

★ St. Andrew's United Methodist Church Plano, Texas

Plano Balloon Festival takes place each fall.

The Plano S.ymphony is one of the numerous professional musical groups located in Collin County.

Collin County is the home to top professional and amateur sports venues. The Texas League AA minor league baseball team, Frisco RoughRiders play at the award-winning Dr Pepper Ballpark. The McKinney Marshals play at the ball fields in Craig Ranch. The Dallas Stars National Hockey League is headquarted in Frisco and the team practices in the arena there. The Texas Tornado of the North American Hockey Leaque have been based in Frisco since the fall of 2003, and shortly after the NAHL moved its main offices there as well. FC Dallas (formerly the Dallas Burn), a Major League Soccer team moved their home to Pizza Hut Park in Frisco in August 2005. A major international youth soccer tournament, The Dallas Cup, is hosted at the Pizza Hut Park each year and draws teams from around the world. Frisco is also home of the Superdrome, one of the top outdoor velodromes in the nation. McKinney hosts the Mickey Mantle World Series and numerous girls' fast pitch and youth soccer tournaments at the fields in Craig Ranch.

Professional venues, training facilities, as well as many youth and adult leagues for soccer, girls fast-pitch softball, baseball, volleyball, cycling both road and off-road, championship Frisbee golf courses, swimming, tennis, hockey, and gymnastics are among the many opportunities offered for the sports enthusiast. There are over 25 golf courses located in Collin County including the Tournament Players Course located at Craig Ranch.

State recognized high schools located throughout Collin County have produced several state championship teams in football, soccer, tennis, cross-

★

Back to school at John Paul II High School.

country, volleyball, softball, baseball, as well as a variety of other sports while at the same time preparing those students for the future academically.

Collin County embraces technology and tradition. The ability to celebrate the past, while nurturing future growth, has helped make Collin County one of the best places to live in the nation. Remarkable real estate values make it one of the best investment opportunities in the country. Collin County is big

★

Collin County has some of the finest education opportunities to be found in the state.

PHOTO COURTESY OF GUY GIERSCH

This is a sample caption.

enough to have all the shopping you might want. There are several historic downtowns found scattered throughout Collin County. Historic Downtown Plano, Celina, Farmersville, or McKinney, the county seat which has three National Register Historic Districts offer eyes on the past while clearly looking forward to the future. These downtowns are filled with antique shops, one-of-a-kind boutique stores, art galleries, and excellent restaurants. These historic downtowns offer neighborhoods that are distinctive with their main street appeal and walk-to conveniences.

PHOTO COURTESY OF ERIC EPSTEIN

★
Below: Islamic Association of Plano.

★

Prestonwood Baptist Church and Chapel located in Plano.

★
First United Methodist Church in McKinney, Texas was formed in 1851.

The chance to discover new attractions in Collin County never ends. A few of the attractions include: Heard Natural Science Museum and Wildlife Sanctuary, Heritage Farmstead Museum, Interurban Museum, Chestnut Square Historic Village, Collin County History Museum, Collin County Farm Museum, and the Heard-Craig Historic Center. Besides an abundance of museums, Collin County has several performance venues, which offer professional entertainment. Among those venues are the McKinney Performing Arts Center, Heard-Craig Auditorium, Courtyard Theater in Plano, Collin County Community College Theater, and the newly designed "Collin County Performing Arts Center" the site of an arts and education environment to ensure all can share and enjoy the full diversity and vitality of the arts. The "Arts Park" includes performance venues, educational and rehearsal space, visual arts display, outdoor spaces

★

Below: Plano Symphony Orchestra at the Courtyard Theater in Plano, Texas.

★

Chisholm Trail is celebrated in bronze near the Stonebriar Center Mall in Frisco, Texas.

for informal performance, sculpture display, and parking plus hike and bike trails. Collin County is known for the vast park systems and several hundred miles of quality hike and bike trails.

Collin County actively adds new parks and open space resources in order to protect to protect and maintain a balance between developed and open landscape. There is an effort to preserve rare or unique ecosystems. Collin County has a farm museum, the Myers Park & Event Center for various 4H and FFA programs, and an adventure camp in Westminster, a place for hands-on study of natural sciences designed for students. Lake Lavon provides opportunities for boating and fishing enthusiasts. Sister Grove Park is a 75-acre hike/bike trail between Princeton and Farmersville adjacent to Lake Lavon while Bratonia Park is a place for the radio-controlled airplane enthusiast. Trinity Trail is an equestrian and hiking trail with trailheads at Brockdale Park and East Fork Park adjacent to Lake Lavon.

ArtCentre Theatre
CHILDRENS THEATRE
JUL 14 -23 ALADDIN
JUL28 AUG6 WINNIE THE POOH

city of plano
COURTYARD
THEATER

RACE FOR THE CURE
3433
RACE FOR THE CURE
3432

★

Asian American Festival in Plano, Texas.

★ Above: Dr. Pepper Park in Frisco is home to the Frisco Rough Riders.

THE SUSAN G. KOMEN BREAST CANCER FOUNDATION
RACE FOR THE CURE

★

Collin County soccer facilities are among the best in the nation.

★
Hike and bike trails provide outdoor opportunities for the family.

★

Dr. Pepper Star Center in Frisco is the practice ice for the Dallas Stars and numerous hockey leagues of all ages.

★
Access to numerous lakes provide plenty of activities from boating to fishing to leisurely afternoon picnics.

Asian American Heritage Festival

★

Access to numerous lakes provide plenty of activities from boating to fishing to leisurely afternoon picnics.

COORS LIGHT
ENJOY
Shiner
BOCK
Welcome To
SHINER
SUNDAY!

PRICE LIST
REGULAR
HAIR CUT
SEBRING CUT $ 13.00
FLAT TOP $ 13.00
SHAMPOO $ 5.00
BEARD TRIM $ 3.00-6.00
Dr Pepper

★

Whether dancing at 'Love and War in Texas', getting a haircut in McKinney, or eating ice cream at 'Herby's,' life has a nice pace in Collin County.

PHOTO COURTESY OF GUY GIERSCH

★

Collin County has a unique blend of historic shops as well as cutting edge.

A Dynamic Economy

Town centers such as Legacy Town Center and transit villages such as Eastside Village in Plano offer live work opportunities that combine shopping, entertainment, and restaurants to provide an urban lifestyle. Eastside Village is located next door to a Dallas Area Rapid Transit (DART) Station and close to major highways for quick access to work and area amenities.

Transportation routes continue to influence Collin County's growth patterns. Transportation is an important part of growth and sustainability for a community. Highways, rail lines, as well as airports such as the Collin County Regional Airport, home of the Texas Instruments and EDS fleets, have become the connections to deliver and receive goods and services.

State Highway 121 provides a direct link to the Dallas Fort Worth International Airport. U.S. Highway 380 provides a direct link to I-35, the NAFTA superhighway, and Dallas North Tollway, George Bush Turnpike, and

★ Paying homage to the past while connecting to the future.

US 75 are all easily accessible and provide direct connections to the Metroplex and beyond. These highways serve as arteries to the variety of shopping, entertainment and lifestyle venues located in Collin County.

Location, combined with the transportation routes that serve it, have helped make Collin County the richest county in Texas and part of the richest 1% of counties in the United States. The median income for a household in the county was $74,136 as of the last report of the US Census Bureau in 2003. The primary cities in this fast growing county are McKinney, Plano, Allen, Frisco, Wylie, Melissa, Celina, Fairview, Anna, and Farmersville as well as small portions of Dallas and Richardson that are located in Collin County. According to U.S. Census estimates, April 2000 till July 2003 Collin County ranked 13th among the fastest-growing counties in the United States and as of 2006 is still in the top 50. The population of the county grew from

491,774 to 597,147 during the period, a growth rate of 21.4 percent.

Excellent schools, both public and private, can be found throughout Collin County. Branches of Southern Methodist University, University of Dallas, as well as nationally acclaimed Collin County Community College provide post-secondary educational opportunities. According to the Census, 136,630 people in Collin County were enrolled in school in 2000. Countywide, 91.8 percent earned a high school diploma or higher and 47.3 percent earned a bachelor's degree or higher. The equivalent statewide figures for a high school diploma or higher and a bachelor's degree or higher were 75.7 percent and 23.2 percent, respectively. The meteoric growth in population combined with the high level of education has created an atmosphere for great business opportunities. As a result of he opportunities Collin County has become home to many corporate headquarters, including Dr Pepper/Seven Up, Inc., Electronic Data Systems (EDS), Frito-Lay, Cinemark Theatres, and JC Penney as well as several corporations such as Raytheon, Fischer, Encore Wire, and Sage Telecom. The telecom corridor averages 50 technology companies per square mile.

Collin County is a place you can hang your hat. The climate, low cost of living, excellent schools, major transportation systems, creative urban atmospheres have helped create a robust economy. The first-rate educational opportunities, remarkable leisure activities, and affordable, premium housing will continue to stimulate increases in population in cities such as McKinney, Frisco, and Allen. McKinney is expected to reach a projected population of 350,000 within 20 years to become the largest city in Collin County. The ability for Collin County to grow continues to be based on the quality of the land and the opportunities it has yielded.

★

Plano Transit Village located near the DART Station in Downtown Plano.

★ Aerial view of Allen, Texas.

★
Aerial view of US Highway 75 looking from Allen toward McKinney.

★ 16th Street DART Station near downtown Plano.
PHOTO COURTESY OF DART

PHOTO COURTESY OF GUY HIRSCH

★

Above: Ham's Meat Market in Historic Downtown McKinney.

Opposite: Shops at Legacy in Plano.

KHYI 95.3
KHYI 95.3
MIC 2
ViewSonic

SUGAR FREE
Strawberry Rhubarb Preserves
Red Tomato Preserves
NET WT. 20 OZ. (566g)
Red Tomato Preserves
NET WT. 20 OZ. (566g)
Red Tomato Preserves

PLANO
CHAMBER OF COMMERCE

★

Left: Plano Presbyterian Hospital

PHOTO COURTESY OF PLANO PRESBYTERIAN

Below: EDS Corporate headquarters in Plano.

Opposite: Education, lifestyle, and climate encourage and promote the growth of business in Collin County.

LIONS
LIONS
LIONS
LIONS

PARTNERS IN COLLIN COUNTY

Pprofiles of people, businesses, and organizations that have contributed to the development and economic base of Collin County

Craig International

Founded by visionary developer and businessman David Craig, Craig International was created in McKinney with the opening of the company's first office nearly three decades ago. Today, the company's influence is felt worldwide, with offices in Los Angeles, Taiwan, and China.

David's father, James, was a career military man, so the Craig family lived all over the world during David's childhood years. His earliest years were spent in Japan and Germany. At age eleven, the family moved back to the United States and David became involved in sports. He excelled in football, wrestling and boxing, attracting regional and national attention while attending high school in Virginia. After graduating from high school in the mid 1970s, he played running back at Texas A&M, sharing time with All-American Bubba Bean.

His first occupation out of college was that of a sports agent. After a couple years of "babysitting athletes," he decided to try the real estate business. In researching his first real estate purchase, he made the acquaintance of Willie Jack Cuellar and his brothers, co-founders of El Chico Restaurants and many other enterprises across Texas. "Mama's boys," as they were widely known, took a liking to young Craig and taught him about real estate, coaching him through his first few deals.

Not long thereafter, James, then a colonel in the Air Force, was nominated for his first star, the rank of general, but instead chose to join David at Craig Properties (now Craig International), where the two continued to work side-by-side for twenty-two years. While James is no longer a full-timer with the firm, he is still active in its operation.

One of the outstanding properties developed by Craig International was James Island (named after the elder Craig), an 850-acre development in British Columbia, Canada. The property includes a Jack Nicklaus golf course and now serves as a retreat for Microsoft executives. *Forbes* magazine recently rated it as the most expensive private island in the world.

Today, Craig International may be most famous for its development of Craig Ranch. This visionary project actually began over twenty-five years ago, when, with no money and very little know-how, David began negotiating the purchase of a section of land in the McKinney area. Though it hardly looked like the beginnings of entrepreneurial greatness at the time, today the project is what has been aptly described as "[Craig's] most impressive accomplishment to date"—Craig Ranch.

Craig Ranch is the leading example in North Texas of "New Urbanism," the name given to the recent movement promoting creation of diverse, compact, vibrant communities. The development began in September 2000 with the purchase of the first 1,125 acres. It now consists of over 2,000

Tournament Players Club (TPC) at Craig Ranch.

acres where the communities of McKinney, Allen, Plano, and Frisco converge. The area is one of the fastest growing in the country. All of the components of the community, including housing, employment, schools, shopping, and recreation, are found within five to ten minutes of one another. Most are accessible by walking.

Craig had a vision and visited many developments around the world that were using the New Urbanism label. He left everyone thinking that something was missing. Some piece of the pie wasn't there. When planning Craig Ranch, he was determined to make it the "whole pie."

When the PGA Tour approached Craig about building a golf course at Craig Ranch, his initial response was that the land was worth too much. Then, he started considering the value of becoming only the twenty-fifth member of the TPC network, and decided that it was exactly the piece needed to complete the pie. Today, it is the centerpiece of the Craig Ranch development—a $45 million golf course designed by renowned tour player and architect Tom Weiskopf, who is known for his classic-style layouts and hands-on approach. The course includes five sets of tees varying the yardage from the 5,050 of the Forward tees up to the 7,483 of PGA Tour tees, where the course/slope ratings of 77.0/152 make it the most challenging layout in Texas.

No homes will encroach on the golf course. The views in the interior of the course are of nothing but the natural terrain of Rowlett Creek, a meandering, white limestone-based creek that comes into play on eleven of the eighteen holes.

Creating the TPC at Craig Ranch was the largest effort ever undertaken by the PGA Tour, which owns and operates the facility. Club membership is capped at 450 and the annual number of rounds will be limited to 35,000 and maybe even as low as 30,000. Between the limited number of rounds, and employment of ten-minute intervals on tee times, it is unusual for anyone to ever have to wait to hit a shot!

Dr. Kenneth Cooper, known as the "father of aerobics," picked Craig Ranch as the location for his landmark health and fitness center, a $15 million, 76,000-square-foot complex. The fitness center is the starting point for a vision known as "Cooper Living." Residents have access to on-site twenty-four-hour medical care at the touch of a button, unlimited doctor house calls, monitored diets, and much more.

The Ballfields at Craig Ranch include 15 baseball and softball fields on 75 acres, with an accompanying 60,000-square-foot training academy. Craig co-owns, with former major leaguer Michael Henneman, the McKinney Marshals, a Texas Collegiate League team that plays its home games at the complex. Negotiations are being finalized with Olympic

✧

Above: The state-of-the-art facilities of Cooper Aerobics are located on the grounds of Craig Ranch.

Below: The trolley at Craig Ranch.

runner Michael Johnson, who will, for three to six months each year, host athletes from around the world at the training facility as part of his "Ultimate Performance" program.

Craig donated 68 acres on which the City of McKinney built 13 youth premier soccer fields. Adjacent to the soccer fields will be Xstreme Thrills at Craig Ranch, a family-oriented entertainment and water park which includes water rides, miniature golf, go-carts and much more.

Rowlett Creek.

The Medical Center at Craig Ranch, a fifty-three-thousand-square-foot healthcare center, is currently under construction. Khandpur McKinney Investment Group is near breaking ground on a forty-thousand-square-foot Craig Ranch Montessori school in the development. Three hotels are planned. A town center that includes mixed-use residential and retail space is currently under design.

The residential development underway at Craig Ranch includes condominiums, single-family homes, and multimillion dollar estates. It is estimated that, when fully built out, 38,000 people will live in the development and 30,000 will be employed there.

Studies show that Americans do not want to walk for longer than five minutes when going from one place to another, so each location of interest in the development must be within a five-minute walk, or easily accessible via another mode of transportation. The Craig Ranch system of trolleys operates to ferry residents among all of the areas of the development on ten-minute intervals.

When planning a project where the total investment runs into the hundreds of millions of dollars, there obviously needed to be a large degree of certainty that the concept would work. Craig believes that there has been a fundamental shift in American attitudes since the events of 9/11.

People realize that their family is the most important thing in their lives. That realization makes them want to spend more time with their loved ones and less time commuting to and from work. Developments such as Craig Ranch facilitate this by shrinking the radius of one's everyday activities.

Another reason that the concept is working is due to the philanthropic aspect of the development. Because having a high-end, private club in the development might seem at odds with the goals of New Urbanism, Craig wanted to leverage the notoriety of the TPC brand to give back to the community. Hence, the club designates one day of the week for its Monday outings, where non-members can play the course for a reasonable tournament entry fee, and local charities reap the benefits. It fits well with the mission of the PGA Tour of raising money for charitable organizations, and also into Craig's personal philosophy of supporting local philanthropic causes.

Craig says he's proud that the development is in McKinney, a community proclaimed by *Dallas Magazine* as "a beautiful patchwork quilt, made up of many shapes and colors, altogether making it a delightful whole."

It is an area which he has called home practically his entire career. "I'm blessed...and I remember where I came from." That is why he is responsible for $2 to $4 million in local philanthropic causes each year.

Craig's love for McKinney is also evident, as he has honored the area's unique history throughout the Craig Ranch development. A number of street names in The Settlement commemorate those visionary pioneers who were among the areas first inhabitants, including Squeezepenny Lane, which pays tribute to an area that included dozens of Collin County communities and historical events that have long since passed into history; Chief Spotted Tail was the head of a small band of Kiowa Indians who lived just west of the first settlement established by Jack McGarrah at Buckner; Choctaw Lane and Chickasaw Trail are reminders of the Indians who inhabited Collin County; Rowlett Creek is named for Daniel Rowlett who took lands along the creek in 1842; and Trading Post Drive honors those early entrepreneurs who established Collin County's first stores.

According to Craig, the development is still in its infancy. He believes it will be ten years before it reaches "full bloom." In fifteen years, he estimates Craig Ranch will have a $2.9 billion impact annually on the area. Craig says that the development "…is a prototype for what communities need to be in this country. People will work, live, and play here."

A special thanks to writer Grant Lovaasen, Helen Hall and Donald Hoke with the Collin County Historical Society, Inc., for the information contained in this story.

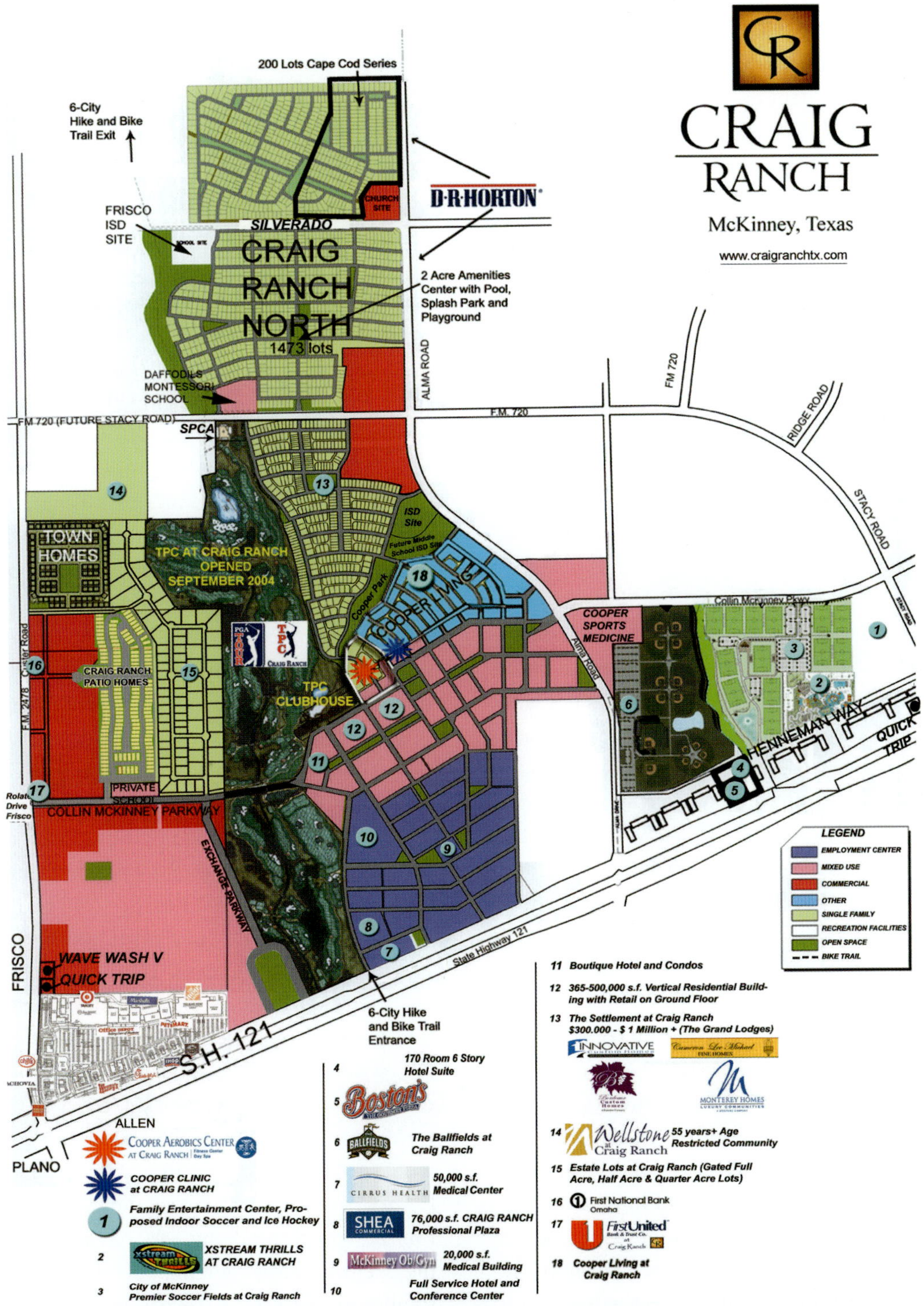

The master plan for Craig Ranch.

Center for Spine Care

Dr. John Peloza

Founded in 1998 by internationally recognized Dallas-based orthopedic surgeon John Peloza, M.D., P.A., the Center for Spine Care is among the foremost treatment centers in the nation, providing state-of-the-art, high quality care for people suffering from back and neck pain.

Motivated by a lifelong passion for spine care and research, Dr. Peloza's focus has been the integration of the very best medical technology with the most current treatments available for back and neck pain. An outstanding staff and team of medical professionals are equally motivated to ensure that every patient is treated as an individual, with individual medical needs that can only be met through a consistent, well-established and high quality level of care and support.

Dr. Peloza, an advisor to the Steadman Hawkins Clinic in Vail, Colorado and the spine consultant to the United States Ski Team, attended the United States Air Force Academy as an Air Force Cadet and received his bachelor's degree from the University of Illinois. After graduating with a medical degree from Northwestern University Medical School, he moved to Dallas to complete his internship and residency at the University of Texas Southwestern Medical Center. It was in his third year as a resident at Texas Scottish Rite Hospital that Dr. Peloza discovered his passion for spine care as he worked with doctors from the United States, France and Germany who were pioneers in the treatment of scoliosis. Later, a Spine Fellowship under Dr. David Selby, a founder of the prestigious North American Spine Society, allowed Dr. Peloza to travel across North America and throughout Europe in a one-year study that focused directly on issues of the spine.

Dr. Peloza is an innovator and pioneer of minimal access spinal technologies (MAST). These revolutionary MAST techniques have dramatically changed the outcome for patients and continue to pave the way for future innovative treatments. Dr. Peloza has participated as an investigator in many FDA clinical trials regarding new spine techniques that address motion technologies including artificial discs, spinal implants, and biologic technologies. These techniques, such as bone morphogenetic protein (a bone growth stimulator which eliminates the need for bone grafts) and artificial disc replacement technology, are just the beginning of what is in store for the future of spine health. Dr. Peloza has authored four book chapters, journal articles, and given over 250 national and international scientific presentations.

Dr. Peloza is an active member of many medical organizations including the International Spine Injection Society, American Medical Association, and American College of Sports Medicine, North American Spine Society, and the American Academy of Orthopedic Surgeons. He served as a member of the Spine Scientific Advisory Board for Sulzer Spine Tech, Inc., and an advisor to Nuvasive Technologies. He is presently an advisor to Medtronic Sofamor Danek, the largest spine technology company in the world. Dr. Peloza is also a member of the Board of Scientific Advisors of K2M, LLC, an incubator for new spine technologies and intellectual property. As an inventor, Dr. Peloza holds a patent for a spinal implant. As a researcher, Dr. Peloza is a member of the Kostuik Research Society as well as a member

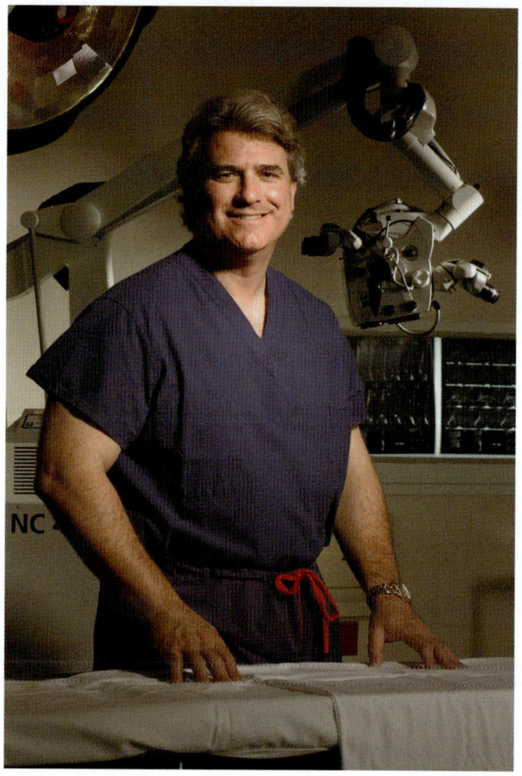

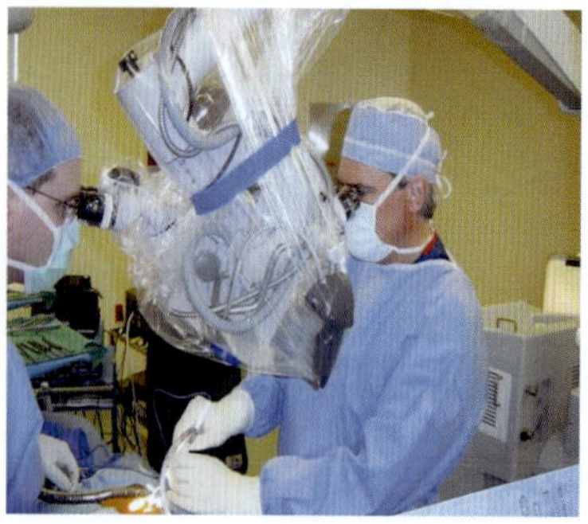

Above: Dr. Peloza in an operating room at Baylor Frisco Medical Center.

Below: Dr. Peloza performing a minimally invasive surgical technique.

of the Lumbar Spine Study Group, a collection of twenty of the top national and international spine surgeons dedicated to advancing scientific knowledge and publications. As a teacher, Dr. Peloza has been an associate professor of orthopaedic surgery at UT Southwestern Medical Center and presently trains spine surgeons nationally and internationally in modern spine surgery.

A longtime advocate of offering options to patients and recommending surgery as a last treatment method, Dr. Peloza is an authority regarding the latest treatment options for the back and spine, due to his active involvement with worldwide medical organizations and participation in national research studies. He has been honored by *D Magazine* as a "Best Doctor in Dallas" for several years and has consistently been named in "Best Doctors in America," the gold standard of physician quality. *The Consumer's Research Council of America Guidebook* has also honored Dr. Peloza as a "Top Surgeon in America."

Dr. Peloza is a maverick in the spine care field, providing patients with a renewed sense of hope to combat the all-too-common fears that often accompany back and neck pain. Creating the Center for Spine Care's satellite office at Baylor Frisco Medical Center in Frisco was an important step in that evolution. A world-class, five-star facility with an outstanding team of administrators and staff members, the site offers a 3-to-1 patient to nurse ratio and, as Dr. Peloza describes it, an entirely "unhospital-like" atmosphere. The City of Frisco itself is hospitable, easy to get around in, and a beautiful place to work and live.

In less than a decade, the Center for Spine Care has earned an outstanding reputation for its pioneering approach to the treatment of spinal disorders. With an emphasis on minimally invasive procedures, the Center offers a multitude of advanced medical and surgical treatment options including pain blocks, physical therapy, medications, injections and minimally invasive endoscopic techniques. Complex reconstructive spine procedures are also available for failed spine surgery, spinal tumors and spinal infections.

The Center for Spine Care is located at Physicians Medical Center in Dallas and along Warren Parkway at Baylor Frisco Medical Center in Frisco. For more information about the Center's innovative care and treatment options, visit www.centerforspinecare.com.

✧

Above: Dr. John Peloza.

Below: Dr. Peloza with his family: son, John, Jr., wife, Renee, and daughter, Samantha.

K. Hovnanian Homes

The Goodman Family of home builders has offered a rich legacy of quality homes and outstanding customer service to Dallas/Fort Worth for more than twenty-five years.

When it was acquired by K. Hovnanian Homes in 1999, the company joined the ninth largest homebuilder in the United States and, according to *Fortune* magazine, one of the 100 fastest growing companies in the country.

With a national reputation as one of the most respected homebuilders in the country and more than 185,000 homes sold in seventeen states, K. Hovnanian Homes has continued Goodman's strong commitment to service across the Metroplex. In late 2005 the Goodman Family of Builders, which includes Westminster Homes, Diamond Homes and Goodman Custom Homes, formally changed its name to K. Hovnanian Homes.

Formed by Kevork S. Hovnanian in 1959 with the debut of thirty-nine single-family homes in Toms River, New Jersey, he envisioned a homebuilding company that would provide lasting value for its homeowners for many years to come. Now in its second generation of family leadership, K. Hovnanian Homes operates with the resources of a solid national company yet retains its proficiency and distinctiveness in local markets.

In the 1970s the company began focusing on active-adult communities, while second home and investment condominiums were emphasized in the early 1980s and included town homes and condominiums for the first-time home buyer. The 1990s brought an increased demand for detached single-family homes and Goodman Custom Homes became a part of the company in 1999.

Committed to creating distinctive custom home environments and lasting value for more than two decades, K. Hovnanian's philosophy has been centered on personal attention and unparalleled service. From concept to completion, every customer enjoys a relationship with the company's experienced builders and award-winning architects. A team of specialists creates an environment that is rich in texture, style, and sophistication.

The purchase of a K. Hovnanian home ensures that customers are not only investing in a house, but also establishing a lifestyle. Each home is located in a premier community, designed to take full advantage of the natural surroundings and streetscapes, and includes a beautiful custom landscaping package.

Thorough inspections at each phase of construction guarantee that detailed workmanship and building techniques for every home are of the finest quality. A

high sales volume, coupled with the large number of new communities and relationships with industry professionals, enables the company to purchase the best materials from the most reliable sources, assuring the best possible value.

K. Hovnanian's pledges to pursue excellence at every level as employees meet the customer's needs. Associates are available to answer questions and make sure that each step of the home buying process meets the buyer's expectations. The truest measure of customer satisfaction are the many families now living in their second, third and even fourth K. Hovnanian home.

K. Hovnanian's Four Seasons Active Adult Communities set the standard for lifestyle, fulfillment and value. Ideally located, these unique resort-at-home communities provide a private world where friendships flourish, recreation abounds and quality is second to none.

Though it began as a family-owned business, with well-defined acquisition efforts, K. Hovnanian Homes has expanded to become a family of homebuilders with localized expertise in numerous markets throughout the United States. Jimmy Brownlee currently serves as president of the company's Dallas/Fort Worth region and Kim Tullos operates as the area marketing director. Today, revenues exceed $5 billion with more than 16,000 homes delivered annually. Additionally, for the fourth year in a row, the company has been recognized as one of *Fortune*'s 100 Fastest Growing Companies, most recently rated at sixty-fourth.

Offering clients more than a half-century of trusted experience in creating the finest homes, it is little wonder that K. Hovnanian Homes remains the First Name in Lasting Value.

For more information regarding K. Hovnanian Homes, which is located at 5808 West Plano Parkway in Plano, Texas, visit the website at www.khov.com and see what they have to offer you and your family.

Presbyterian Hospital of Plano

Presbyterian Hospital of Plano opened its doors in 1991 with the mission of improving the healthcare of those in the communities it serves. Today, the 370-bed, not-for-profit, faith-based community hospital serves a yearly volume of more than 115,000 patients.

Plano has changed dramatically since the hospital opened in what was then an unpopulated location in far West Plano. Today, residential neighborhoods, businesses, and the Dallas North Tollway embrace the fifty-eight-acre campus. The hospital serves the healthcare needs of families and corporate employees in far north Dallas, Collin, and Denton Counties.

Presbyterian Hospital of Plano, which is accredited by the Joint Commission on Accreditation of Healthcare Organizations, lists more than 1,100 medical staff members and is recognized for offering all private rooms. All of the hospital's employees, volunteers, and physicians are dedicated to providing quality healthcare in a caring environment.

Founded on a tradition of excellence, Presbyterian Hospital of Plano has earned a reputation for advanced facilities, personal care and an unsurpassed staff of medical professionals representing a multitude of specialties. Services include assisted reproductive technology services (ARTS), cardiovascular, critical care, emergency, pediatric, rehabilitation, surgical, women's and children's, and more. The ARTS program was named one of the Top 10 Fertility Centers in the United States by *Child* magazine.

Above: Phil Wentworth, FACHE, president, Presbyterian Hospital of Plano.

Below: Aerial photo of Presbyterian Hospital of Plano c. 2006.

In 1997, the hospital broke ground on a massive $86.7 million expansion, adding a new five-story hospital wing in addition to a third medical office building. The expansion was the largest construction project in the city at that time and one of North Texas' most significant hospital expansions of the decade. It increased hospital capacity to 174 beds, boosted operating rooms by more than seventy percent, expanded emergency facilities by fifty-six percent and nearly doubled the area for labor, delivery and recovery.

Additions included a dedicated orthopedic and neurology surgery unit, a neonatal intensive care unit (NICU) Level III nursery, a new cardiac catherization lab, the Sue A. de

Mille Woman's Diagnostic Center and extended major surgical capabilities, including open heart and vascular procedures. The newly expanded obstetrics unit holds a 56-bed postpartum area, a 20-bed high-risk obstetrics ante partum area, and a 17-bed labor and delivery area.

"The expansion of our hospital is a direct response to the current and anticipated needs of the community," says President Phil Wentworth. Wentworth, who has led the hospital since 1993, adds that, "Everything we have planned will have a direct benefit for our current patient population and prepare us for realistic future needs of the relatively young, growing, dynamic community."

Presbyterian Hospital of Plano is guided by a non-compensated, interdenominational board of trustees composed of community leaders, physicians, and people dedicated to quality healthcare.

The hospital continues to expand in order to meet the ever growing and changing needs of Collin and Dallas Counties. The Sue A. de Mille Tower, part of the hospital's $120.9 million expansion project, houses the Cardiac Interventional Unit, Emergency, Intensive Care Unit (ICU), Medical-Surgery, NICU, and Postpartum areas.

This construction project includes an expanded 24,000 square foot Emergency Department that is Collin County's largest, with four trauma rooms, 27 sub-specialty treatment rooms, and 20 fast-track (minor care) rooms. A new parking lot with thirty-one dedicated spaces is available for Emergency Room parking. All treatment rooms are private.

In addition, the new tower includes a twenty-six-bed Intensive Care Unit with the latest technology to monitor even the most seriously ill patients, and a Neonatal Intensive Care Unit that combines advanced technology with specialized care for the tiniest of patients. The expanded neonatal unit features an aquatic Noah's Ark theme. With forty-five beds, it is one of the largest NICUs in Collin County and treats more than five hundred infants each year.

Centrally located on the hospital campus, the nine-story de Mille Tower features windowed lobbies overlooking Parker Road. Immediately below these lobbies is a garden with blooming flowers, evergreen plants, flowering trees, five fountain jets and a peaceful river-rock stream lined with decorative gravel. Park benches and shade trees provide patients and guests with a place to relax and enjoy being outside. This garden entrance provides access to a newly built two-story concourse that connects all hospital buildings and the expanded parking garage to the de Mille Tower. The tower is named for a local philanthropist, Sue A. de Mille.

In partnership with local institutions, organizations and corporations, Presbyterian routinely hosts health and wellness fairs, immunization clinics, and other health-related programs free of charge to the community.

The hospital is a member of Texas Health Resources (Presbyterian Healthcare System and Harris Methodist Healthcare System), one of the largest not-for-profit, faith-based health networks in the United States. The thirteen-hospital system is the largest in North Texas in terms of patients served and includes Harris Methodist Hospitals, Arlington Memorial Hospital and Presbyterian Healthcare System.

For more information, please visit the website at www.phscare.org.

Jerry Madden

District Sixty-seven Representative Jerry Madden is dedicated in many areas; but his first and foremost loyalty goes to his family. A father to three adult children, Jerry, Stephanie and Kristina and grandfather to six, Madden and his wife Barbara, a nurse, have been married forty years.

His son followed in his dad's military footsteps and is a major in the Army in Germany. Stephanie, her husband and children live in Tampa, Florida. His other daughter, Kristina, is following her dad's career as an insurance agent in his Plano office of the Jerry Madden Insurance firm. Dedicated to his business in insurance sales, Madden provides life and health plan insurance coverage to individuals and businesses.

Upon graduation from West Point with a Bachelor of Science in Engineering, Madden spent six years in the Army, including one year in Vietnam and two years in Germany, before bringing his family to Richardson in 1971. He worked eleven years for Texas Instruments, eight years for Teledyne Geotech and obtained a Master of Science in Management and Administration Sciences from the University of Texas at Dallas in 1979. Madden went into insurance sales in 1994 and opened his own agency in 2000.

Madden's insurance agency has five employees. He oversees his legislative office staff and committee staff in Plano and Austin.

Above: Texas Representative Jerry Madden legislates with the best interests of his Collin County constituents at heart.

Below: Representative Madden (Center)and his wife Barbara (left), and Barbara's mother, Bernice Szumachowski (right).

Madden takes each of his roles very seriously and realizes that dedication is required in each area of his responsibility.

He also views himself as a dedicated politician. He is serious about his role as an elected official. Madden was reared in a family with strong political values. His father was an elected clerk in the municipal court in Council Bluff, Iowa. When he left the job to go off to WWII, Madden's mother was appointed to take his place while he served the country. She held that elected clerk position for almost sixteen years.

Madden has been involved in Collin County politics since they moved here. Dedicated to the Republican philosophy, he was elected Precinct Chairman in his local neighborhood in 1974 and Chairman of the Republican Party of Collin County in 1984.

"Today, I am in a fortunate place of being a statesman, not just running for office. I can put a lot of the politics aside and try to do what I call statesmanship," he said. First elected to the Texas Legislature in November of 1992 and now in his seventh term, Madden serves on the House Committees on Civil Practices and is chairman of the House Committee on Corrections.

As the chairman of the Corrections Committee for the State of Texas, Madden has the responsibility with the committee for

◇

State Representative Madden joins the Seventy-eighth Legislative Staff and Interns including; Chief of Staff Karin Lim Tucker (4th from the left); Corrections Committee staff member, Steven Schar (6th from the left); Corrections Committee staff member, Ren Nance (3rd from the right); staff member Taryn Dusek (2nd from the right); and Legislator Director Mark Hey (far right).

oversight of all the state's prisons, probation programs, parole programs, and criminal correctional facilities. They have a large spectrum of things that they do and he is involved in all of those.

Madden said, "In my legislative career, I have been involved in election law. I have been involved in state affairs, which takes into account all the fraud spectrum of the state. I have been involved in a lot of different things over the years and I still am. I wrote the judicial campaign finance bill that controls all the judicial campaigns of the state, as far as financing and reporting and requirements."

Prior committee appointments have included State Affairs, Calendars, the Select Committee on Public School Finance, Urban Affairs, Public Safety, Elections, State, Federal and International Relations, and Rules and Resolutions.

After every legislative session he has been recognized by one or more organizations for his hard work and dedication. The issues and the legislation for which he has been commended range from driver education to military voting, from parental notification of classroom waivers to judicial campaign fairness, and from electronic filing to nursing home reform.

He has been honored for his work in a variety of policy areas by organizations including the American Legion-Department of Texas, Dallas Chapter of the National Federation of Republican Assemblies, Campaigns for People, Texas Common Cause, Texas Association of Business, Texas Library Association, the Lone Star Foundation, Texas Home School Association, Texas Eagle Forum, American Family Association of Texas and Texas Citizens for a Sound Economy.

He received Special Recognition from the Texas Classroom Teachers Association for his work in education during the 75th, 76th, and 77th Legislatures. He has been rated one of the most conservative state legislators during each of the biennial sessions in which he has served, ranking among the top ten percent most conservative legislators in 1995, 1999 and 2001.

As a thirty-five year resident of Collin County, Jerry has been involved in numerous veterans' and community organizations, holding positions such as President of the Collin County School Board, and Chairman of the Collin County Hospital Board, as well as serving on the Advisory Board of the Plano Chamber of Commerce. He was instrumental in launching the Collin County Caring for Children program, a joint venture between Blue Cross/Blue Shield of Texas and the private sector.

Jerry Madden continues to exhibit the commitment and drive which he first brought to the Legislature. Always accessible to his constituents and sensitive to the changing needs of Texas and District Sixty-Seven Representative Madden seeks to promote limited government, fiscal responsibility, safe and thriving communities and successful families and businesses.

Collin Services, Inc.

Jerry and Margaret Wassom, c. November 2005.

Collin Services, Inc., a full-service pest and termite control company located on Avenue K in Plano, has served the Collin County area since 1972. Locally owned and operated by the Wassom family, Collin Services, Inc. specializes in pest management for residential, commercial, and industrial structures.

The mission of Collin Services, Inc. has always been the Golden Rule, "Do onto others as you would have them do onto you," and the owners say that will never change. Founder Jerry Wassom and his wife, Margaret, who still help manage daily operations, pride themselves in offering courteousness, kindness, and professionalism to all of their customers.

Wassom started Collin County Pest Control as a part-time business from his home in Plano. At the time, he worked at the Plano post office and worked part-time for two pest control companies. "I decided if they could be successful, I could do the same thing. So I started Collin County Pest Control in 1972 and we didn't even have a business phone," he says.

After taking and passing the state license exam, the business started to grow by word of mouth. In September 1973 the company's new phone number came out in the directory and the rest is history. The company name was changed to Collin Services, Inc. in 1992.

Collin Services, Inc.'s success is attributed to two factors: the leadership and vision of its founders, and the talent and dedication of the employees. The first employee was hired in 1982 and today there are eighteen on staff. The Wassoms are proud that their employees enjoy working with the company for many years. Two of their long-time employees are Jerry Spears, eighteen years, and Butch Baldwin, thirteen years.

All of the Wassom children have been involved in the business, from working part-time while in high school and college to making it a full-time career today. The oldest daughter, Shanna, is the office manager and has worked for the company nineteen years. Mitchell, a former football coach and teacher, has been company president since 1990. Rhonda, the younger daughter, is a teacher, but has spent many hours working in the office. Daughter-in-law, Beth, and granddaughter, Audra, have also worked for the company.

Collin Services, Inc. treats pest control as a science. Knowledge of pests, their behavior and habits is essential in solving customer's problems and the firm's professionals are trained to correctly identify the pests, and how to treat for them. All technicians and certified applicators are registered and licensed.

Pest control operators at Collin Services, Inc., are trained in basic entomology, laws, safety, pesticide safety, integrated pest management and more. They focus on what is best for the client and provide the service promised. They provide complete pest control, including termite inspections, pre-treatment of new homes, and treatment of infestations.

As more land is developed in Collin County for the expansion of homes and

businesses, wild animals often show up on resident's doorsteps. To help clients cope with the critters, Collin Services, Inc. has added animal trapping and bird control to its list of services. The company's experts have trapped foxes, skunks and possums and carried them back to the country where they have room to roam.

Collin Services, Inc. provides pest services and mold prevention from homes to shopping centers throughout the DFW Metroplex. The company also treats yards for fleas and grubs and sprays trees for insects and worms.

The Wassom family believes it is important to give back to their community. Working with churches and nonprofits such as Habitat for Humanity and City House bring them a great deal of pleasure. They are members of the Plano Chamber of Commerce, the Indoor Air Quality Association (IAQA), the Greater Dallas Pest Control Association, the Texas Pest Control Association and the National Pest Management Association.

Mitchell has earned both B.S. and M.Ed. degrees. He is a certified pest control applicator and an IAQA nationally certified mold remediator. He is a past president of the Greater Dallas Pest Control Association and the 2006 vice president of the Texas Pest Control Association.

Collin Services, Inc.'s continued business growth can be attributed in part to the strong housing and business market and economy in Collin County. The company continues to expand its coverage area, while focusing on the commercial and new home construction area.

Pests continue to be a problem throughout Collin County—posing risks to property and health. More and more, citizens are turning to professional pest control to solve their household pest problems. Customers realize that pests are more than merely a nuisance, the potential health threats they pose, as well as the impact they can have on a person's or business' bank account, is enough to motivate anyone to outsource their pest problems.

Once Collin Services, Inc. provides an initial inspection; they can recommend the type of services you may require. These services can help prevent extensive property damage resulting from termites and other wood-destroying insects, and public health threats, such as asthma triggered by allergens.

For more information about Collin Services, Inc., please call the Wassom family at 972-423-3030.

The Collin Services, Inc., staff and ownership, c. November 2005. Top row (from left to right): Sam Board, Keith McKinzie, William Weeks, Chris Klein, Terry Huber, Lee Barnes, and Mike Masters. Middle row: Butch Baldwin, Jerry Spears, Brandon Booth, Don Jones, and Cliff Love. Bottom row: Shanna Merritt, Jerry Wassom, Margaret Wassom, Mitchell Wassom, and Judy Barnhart. Not pictured are Bob Stroud and Cathy Williams.

BAYLOR REGIONAL MEDICAL CENTER AT PLANO

Baylor Health Care System's Regional Medical Center at Plano is a visionary facility that continues to distinguish itself as the premier provider of patient-centered care across the region. Through a faith-based culture of caring service, every effort is made to build a healthier community by providing operational and clinical excellence to every patient.

The Baylor Health Care System was originally founded in 1903 as Reverend George W. Truett, pastor of Dallas' historic First Baptist Church, challenged community leaders to "begin to build a great humanitarian hospital…one to which men of all creeds and those of none may come with equal confidence."

Baylor Regional Medical Center at Plano began on the drawing board as a specialty heart hospital but growing physician interest lead the organization to realize that the need and opportunity was broader than what had been imagined. Baylor went back to the drawing board and determined what could be built with the physical space, physician interest and resources available. The result is the Baylor Plano campus, a healing environment dedicated to patient-centered care, which opened its doors to Collin County and the surrounding communities on December 1, 2004.

Today, Baylor Regional Medical Center at Plano continues to be an acute care medical and surgical facility specializing in meeting the healthcare needs of adults. Over eight hundred board-certified physicians and active staff members, as well as over six hundred employees, provide comprehensive diagnosis, treatment, rehabilitation and follow-up care to meet the growing needs of the community. Highly specialized clinical services include internal medicine, gastroenterology, neurology, dermatology, pulmonology, orthopedics, medical and radiation oncology, women's services and cardiology.

Baylor Plano includes 96 inpatient beds, 32 day-surgery patient beds, 12 operating rooms, a full-service, 24-hour emergency department, four cardiac catheterization, electrophysiology and interventional labs, and two endoscopy suites. Adjacent to the hospital, the nearly 189,000 square-foot, eight-floor Baylor Medical

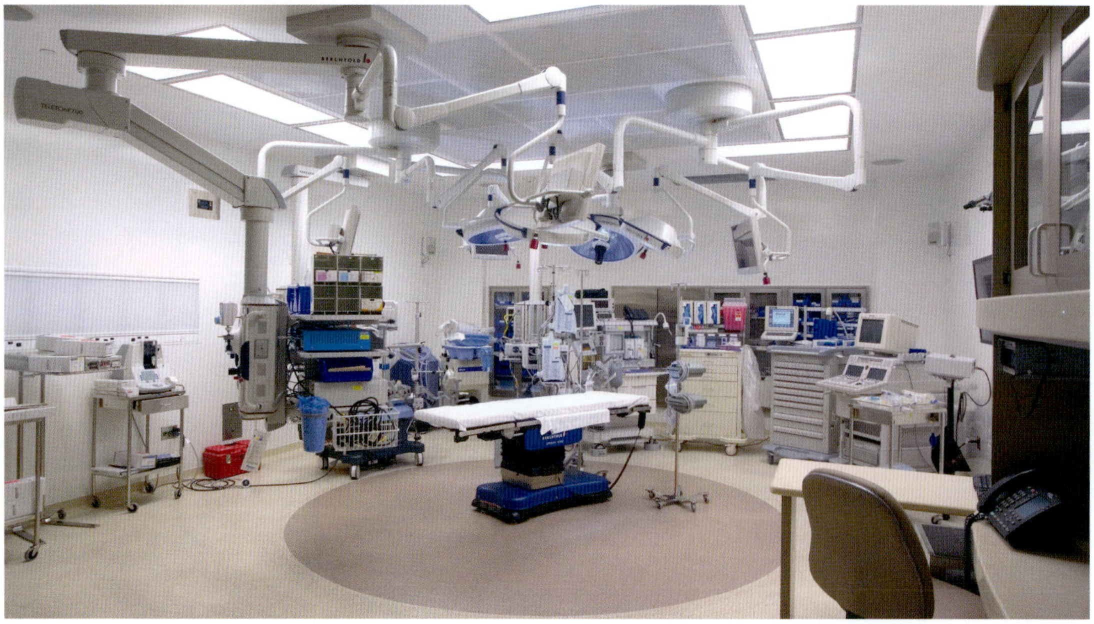

✧

Above: Large windows allow for natural light throughout Baylor Regional Medical Center at Plano and attention to landscaping enhances the grounds and complements the interior décor.

Below: Baylor Regional Medical Center at Plano's large operating rooms offers advanced technology.

Pavilion I houses a full range of primary care physicians and medical specialists.

As part of the Baylor Health Care System, Baylor Plano offers access to innovative treatments and clinical trials performed through the Baylor Research Institute in areas such as oncology and cardiovascular services. In addition, the Baylor Plano campus is home to The Heart Hospital Baylor Plano, the first dedicated heart hospital in Collin County.

Advanced diagnostic and communication technology plays a vital role in the daily lives and well being of patients at Baylor Plano. Physicians are able to digitally display, archive and transmit images such as X-rays, computerized tomography (CT) and magnetic resonance imaging (MRI). This sophisticated technology offers immediate access to images and other medical records, instant verification of image quality, ability to manipulate images for better viewing, efficient delivery, storage, duplication, and the ability to conduct online consultations with other physicians. Advanced digital imaging capabilities include MRI, CT, nuclear medicine and ultrasound. The Baylor Women's Imaging Center offers all-digital imaging, including mammography and osteoporosis screenings. The Baylor Scoliosis Center, located in Medical Pavilion I on the Baylor Plano campus, is devoted to treating advanced spine curvature in both adults and children.

Baylor Plano patients and their families enjoy an array of amenities. Patients stay in private, larger than average hospital rooms designed with warm colors, art and soft lighting. The rooms feature wireless Internet connection and thirty-inch LCD televisions that display patient care information. A gourmet chef prepares meals to the patient's preference and according to physician orders. Additionally, hotel-like room service is available. The design of patient floors also is more amenable for patients and their families. Each floor offers a family lounge complete with a kitchen. Family members are welcome to stay overnight on a comfortable bed in the patient's room.

Baylor Health Care System has always been characterized by its tradition of community service and Baylor Plano is no exception. Community programs are aimed at getting people healthy and helping them stay healthy. Priorities include preventing injuries, cardiovascular disease, diabetes and promoting general wellness. Programs include screenings at community health fairs, local presentations by medical and health professionals, educational seminars and support groups.

Baylor Plano also financially supports several local not-for-profit agencies including the Plano Independent School District Foundation, Collin County Community College Education Foundation, Collin County Children's Advocacy Center, Volunteer Center of Collin County, Junior League of Plano, Maurice Barnett Geriatric Wellness Center, North Texas Affiliate for the Susan G. Komen Breast Cancer Foundation, MS Society and Live From Plano. Additionally, Baylor Plano supports Plano Chamber of Commerce events and the Leadership Plano program.

Baylor Regional Medical Center at Plano is located at 4700 Alliance Boulevard in Plano. For more information about the medical center, please visit www.baylorhealth.com.

Above: Nurses' stations are in close proximity to patient rooms and include technology to aid in patient care.

Below: Baylor Plano nurses celebrate National Nurses week.

North Texas Tollway Authority

The first railroad came to Collin County in the 1870s and, almost instantly, the county blossomed from a sparsely populated region of isolated farms scattered across the Blackland Prairie into a vibrant locale with growing communities and a broadened economic base.

As the railroad represented accessibility, mobility, and opportunity for Collin County settlers in the early days, the Dallas North Tollway System provides those benefits to residents today.

The Dallas North Tollway System (which includes the Dallas North Tollway, President George Bush Turnpike, Addison Airport Toll Tunnel, and Mountain Creek Lake Bridge) is under control of the North Texas Tollway Authority (NTTA), a political subdivision of the State of Texas. The NTTA is the successor to the Texas Turnpike Authority, the state agency that constructed the Dallas Fort Worth Turnpike, now known as IH-30, in the 1950s. That landmark highway introduced high-speed, nonstop travel between its namesake cities and facilitated their rise as a combined economic powerhouse.

The North Texas Tollway Authority was created in 1997 and authorized to acquire, construct, maintain, and operate turnpike projects in the North Texas region. A seven-member Board of Directors including representatives from Dallas, Tarrant, Collin, and Denton Counties governs the NTTA with one adjacent county representative appointed by the Governor of Texas.

The first segment of the Dallas North Tollway opened in 1968. It was subsequently extended in several stages, connecting downtown Dallas with the Park Cities, North Dallas, Addison, and on into the Collin County cities of Plano and Frisco—all towns synonymous with success and buzzing with the excitement of growing opportunities.

A mental journey up the Tollway is a reminder of the remarkable development that has been afforded by this convenient, efficient thoroughfare. The Collin County portion alone traverses an impressive array of retail centers (including The Shops at Willow Bend, the high-end regional shopping mall in Plano), restaurants, entertainment venues, and accommodations. Proximity to the Dallas North Tollway has enabled many major business and employment centers to thrive.

The mission of the NTTA encompasses far more than providing roadway infrastructure. The entire organization is dedicated to relieving traffic congestion and easing headaches for motorists.

The Dallas North Tollway System was the first in the world to introduce TollTag technology, vastly streamlining the process of paying tolls, while reducing the cost for motorists at the same time. Currently, almost one million vehicles in the DFW area are equipped with a TollTag. By 2005, nearly eighty-five percent of Tollway transactions were being processed electronically during peak hours.

To move more traffic, the NTTA has installed express lanes for TollTag users at every toll plaza. The NTTA also works continually to improve customer service for cash customers, reducing the average transaction time to approximately two seconds.

In addition, the NTTA worked diligently with DFW and Dallas Love Field airports to allow the TollTag to be used for pass thru and parking. Agreements with the Harris County Toll Road Authority allow TollTag and EZTag customers to share the convenience of the electronic transponder no matter which city they are in.

The NTTA contributes to the well being of the community in many ways. Among its 700 employees are the staff at the Administrative Offices and Customer Service Center at 5900 West Plano Parkway and the Maintenance Service Center at 1080 Ohio Drive in Plano, and more than 400 Toll Collection employees spread out over fifty-four miles of roads in the DFW region. These front line employees represent the face of the NTTA with pride and dedication.

The NTTA sponsors numerous activities including Live from Plano (a variety show that benefits five local charities), Toys for Tots, AmericaCares (a fundraiser for wounded soldiers home from the Middle East), and Carter Blood Care blood drives. It is also a sponsor of Frisco Safety Town, an interactive and educational mini-community.

As the growth and opportunities of Collin County continue at full speed, the North Texas Tollway Authority is at the forefront. In 2005, a ten-mile extension of Dallas North Tollway from Gaylord Parkway in Frisco north to US 380 was underway with plans in place to extend all the way to Grayson County. The area served by this extension includes Frisco Square and the new Frisco City Hall. And plans are in place for the next phase that will extend the Dallas North Tollway even further. Other projects in various stages of development include the Trinity Parkway west of downtown Dallas, Southwest Parkway in Tarrant County, and the Lewisville Lake Toll Bridge. Working closely with the Collin County Commissioners Court, the cities, elected officials and the Texas Department of Transportation, the NTTA has been able to contribute a vital role in providing improved mobility for Collin County.

The communities spread throughout Dallas, Tarrant, Collin, Denton, and Grayson Counties were once on far-off horizons. But from the earliest days, Texans have always found a way to reach those distant horizons. The NTTA's commitment to the DFW Region is exemplified by its growth and success in Collin County.

Further information about the North Texas Tollway Authority is available at www.ntta.org.

Encore Wire Corporation

A leader in low-cost manufacturing of copper electrical building wire and cable, Encore Wire is a major supplier of both residential wire for interior electrical wiring in homes, apartments and manufactured housing, and commercial wire for electrical distribution in commercial and industrial buildings. Originally a Delaware corporation, McKinney has been home to the company since its principal executive office and plant were opened here at incorporation in 1989.

A native of Rhode Island, Encore's Chairman Vincent Rego first came to Texas with his wife, Dorothy, in 1953 after moving to a new wire plant in Plano. He quickly found his niche in the trade and never tired of seeing his dreams become a reality. Soon recognized as an innovative leader and outstanding force within the wire industry, he and his team bought and sold a wire company in the area before setting their sights upon a "rundown mobile home plant" about thirty-five miles north of Dallas on ten acres in McKinney. Rego's team bought the site, with a truck well and shipping dock, and formed Encore Wire in 1989. Engineer Phil Pringle and current President Daniel Jones were among the first to join the small staff as they eagerly set to work in the sixty-eight-thousand-square-foot building.

Encore strictly offered residential wire as a short-line producer until 1994, when the board approved the growing company's $15-million expansion into a second plant. Now a full-line producer, the company quickly set the standard for innovation, customer service, and high quality within the competitive industry.

Electrical contractors and distributors from around the country have come to appreciate one of Encore's most important innovations in the wire industry—color-coated, commercial feeder wire. The colored wire ensures that electrical contractors install commercial wire safely and efficiently in accordance with National Electrical Codes. High visibility labeling also allows the consumer to easily identify wire types and sizes at a glance, from any angle.

Encore is in the forefront of the development and construction of equipment that enables the company to manage every stage of wire manufacturing—from production, warehousing, shipping, to support processes.

As Encore has grown to become one of the most successful businesses of its kind in the nation, it continues to set a high mark in meeting the demands of distributors with uniquely quick shipping and delivery capabilities. The company emphasizes personal responsibility and accuracy in order and packing procedures, while they consistently maintain an exceptional ninety-

The world's largest Stohlberger Cabling Machine.

nine percent plus order fill rate and therefore create fewer backorders and minimize operational problems and administrative costs.

Since 1990, Encore Wire Limited (an affiliate of Encore Wire Corporation) has built its success with a firm focus on customer service. A philosophy of "select service" remains Encore's standard for success. The company continues to offer one-stop sourcing for residential and commercial building wire needs. Inventory levels remain "broad and deep" and characterize a well established, strong customer loyalty, rapidly handling customer inquiries, orders, and shipments.

Encore is publicly traded on the NASDAQ market as "WIRE" and has been recognized throughout the industry with numerous product and service awards, including Showstopper Awards for the National Electrical Contractors' Association (NECA) as well as the EC&M and CEE News Electrical Product of the Year.

In the second quarter of 2006, Frank Bilban, Encore's vice president and chief financial officer announced the company's quarterly record for net sales at $362 million. In November 2004, Encore Wire received awards for "Supplier of the Year" and "Excellence in Service and Delivery" from the IMARK Group, a large national marketing group of electrical distributors in which members rate all suppliers' performances.

Commenting on his company's outstanding success and looking with great optimism toward the future, Rego said, "There is no substitute for setting high goals and working hard every day to achieve them. Our staff is dedicated to being the best supplier in the electrical industry by exceeding customer expectations. We will continue to focus on these important criteria in addition to innovating new wire products and maintaining strong personal relationships with our valued customers as we continue to grow Encore Wire in the future."

It is indeed a bright future for Encore. Additional information may be obtained by visiting www.encorewire.com.

Above: Encore's Rodmill Plant.

Below: An aerial view of Encore's facilities.

Texas Oncology, P.A.

The largest private practice of physicians dedicated exclusively to cancer care, Texas Oncology, P.A. is committed to historic leadership and unprecedented excellence in oncology care for patients and families across the country and around the world.

This commitment is characterized by the pioneering efforts of its founders—Merrick Reese, M.D.; John Bagwell, M.D.; J. R. Williams, M.D.; Skip Duncan, M.D.; Lloyd Kitchens, Jr., M.D.; Steve Paulson, M.D.; David Snyder, M.D.; and Charles White, III, M.D.—and the groundbreaking care of its renowned medical staff, who now assist more new cancer patients than any other institution in the country.

Though the organization was officially founded on September 30, 1986, it actually began in 1975 with the merger of two practices that included five medical oncologists practicing at Baylor University Medical Center in Dallas, Texas. In 1976, outreach efforts began in Paris, Corsicana and Midland/Odessa. In 1983, the first bone marrow transplant program was established at BUMC. In 1988, Texas Oncology built its first cancer center, which now consists of thirty-five centers. By 1993 there were a total of seventy-three physicians—sixty medical oncologists, four gynecological oncologists, and nine radiation oncologists.

Texas Oncology's steadfast pledge of service to its cancer patients is realized in a number of ways: clinical research and treatment protocols to develop innovative approaches in the science of oncology and hematology that lead to better outcomes and high quality of treatment; high standards for patient satisfaction, established through comprehensive treatment, patient education and interaction with our communities; and value in oncology care by helping patients achieve the best quality of life possible through treatment close to home near the support of family and friends.

The name Texas Oncology is synonymous with "care you would travel for, but don't have to." The organization has grown approximately ten percent annually in its number of physicians, while new patient growth continues at five percent per year. New cancer center growth is at about one to two per year over the past four to five years. Such steady growth is directly related to the organization's focus upon offering the best cancer care through its doctors and technology, access and convenience, minimum wait time, a community setting that is close to home and provides caregivers who live in the area, and access to state-of-the-art research without having to leave home to get it.

The continued success of Texas Oncology has been ably directed through the outstanding leadership of many. Merrick Reese, M.D., served as president and chairman of the board from 1986 to 1998 and developed the hub/spoke growth of cancer providers during the early days of Texas Oncology; Fred Ekery, M.D., served as president and chairman of the board from 1998 to 2000; Steve Paulson, M.D., has served as president and chairman of the board since 2000; Ernie Sims, who has served as the executive director of Texas Oncology since 1987; and Charles White, III, M.D., and Louis Muzon, M.D.

Among the numerous local market and national charities and organizations supported by Texas Oncology and its staff are the American Cancer Society, the Leukemia Association of North Central Texas, St. Paul's Children's Foundation, the Susan G. Komen Race for the Cure, Team Nuts, the Texas Alliance for Patient Access, and the Texas Partnership for End of Life Care.

Texas Oncology is headquartered at 12221 Merit Drive, Suite 500 in Dallas, Texas, and is located on the Internet at www.usoncology.com.

Texas Oncology operates two oncology centers in Abilene; in Amarillo; a cancer center and oncology center in Arlington; two oncology centers and a cancer center in Austin; in Baytown; an oncology center and the Mamie McFadden Ward Cancer Center in Beaumont; an oncology center, the Edward Cancer Center and The Breast Care Center of North Texas in Bedford; in Bonham; Texoma Cancer Center in Bowie; in Breckenridge; South Texas Cancer Center in Brownsville; in Carrollton and Corsicana; three hospitals, three cancer centers, and one oncology center in Dallas; Denison; two oncology centers in Denton; Durant; Eastland; two cancer centers in El Paso; Ennis; three oncology centers in Fort Worth; Frisco; Gainesville; Garland; Grapevine; Greenville; South Texas Cancer Center in Harlingen; four locations in Houston; three centers in Irving; Jacksonville; Jasper; Katy; La Grange; Southern New Mexico Cancer Center in Las Cruces, New Mexico; Lewisville; Longview; Luling; McAllen; McKinney; Mesquite; Mexia; Allison Cancer Center at Midland; Mt. Pleasant; North Richland Hills; West Texas Cancer Center in Odessa; Palestine; Paris; North Texas Regional Cancer Center and an oncology center in Plano; Round Rock; Sherman; Sugarland; Sulphur Springs; Sweetwater; Taylor; Texas City; Tyler; Vernon; Texas Oncology Cancer and Research Center in Waco; Waxahachie; Deke Slayton Cancer Center in Webster; Weslaco, and Texoma Cancer Center in Wichita Falls.

McAndrews Bookshop and Café

One half block from McKinney's Town Square at 115 South Kentucky, Collin County had a prison. Most towns just had a jail, but this fortress was the work of F. E. Ruffini and was completed in 1880. When Stephanie McAndrews first saw this building after moving to McKinney, she knew she had to have it. It blended perfectly with her dream to own a bookstore and café.

Last used as a prison in 1979, and the location of Texas' last hanging, the building had gone through a massive remodeling and been used for several other ventures. She thought that the prison's history filled with stories of outlaws and hangings would be a perfect home to McAndrews Bookshop and Café.

Stephanie's dream came true Christmas 2003, when her husband presented her with the building. Starting in January, they began the remodeling project. Wanting to get the building back to its original state, they sandblasted the walls and got them back to their original 1880-era state. Then working with the Historical Society in Austin, they preserved the walls and began painting and freshening the rooms.

The prison's former exercise area outside was just a flat slab, so they added an arbor and a foundation for the whole patio. A beautiful fireplace is a focal point of the area and brings warmth to chilly Texas evenings.

McAndrews Bookshop and Café opened their doors on October 25, 2004. Stephanie describes the business as an espresso bar and a bookshop. She chose the term "shop" because it is older than "store" matching the age of the building—it is a bookshop with new books. They keep current with all of the best sellers, including hardcover books. McAndrews also carries a Western section in keeping with Texas history. Lovely gift books, beautiful journals, little box sets, and bookmarks are some of the smaller items available.

Fiction books are located on the first floor with their full espresso bar and baristas who can make anything you like. The coffee bean of choice is Illy, a very popular, smooth Italian roast that renders perfect espresso and wonderful coffee. All coffee recipes include an extra espresso shot at no additional charge. They offer a full range of decaf options, and more than twenty flavors can be added to any latte or cappuccino. Sugar-free choices include vanilla, hazelnut, almond and caramel.

To customize your drink, customers can choose among several types of milk or soy. From mochas and caramel machiatos to the best chai ever, they have mastered them all. If you are longing for a classic, they specialize in old favorites: hot chocolate, good conversation, cider, anecdotes, hot tea, personal attention, and even soda. Finally, any drink can be made hot or on ice. Want something even colder? How about a delicious custom smoothie? Every drink is made fresh to your specifications. Pastries and desserts are served all day.

McAndrews has an incredible Children's section. The store offers a special selection to young readers in the fourth and fifth grades. Younger readers, including babies, toddlers, and preschoolers through third and fourth grade series, have their own selection. Millie the Eight-Foot-Ostrich lives in the second-floor Children's Room with several just-right-sized leather rocking chairs and hundreds of all-new books with well-loved titles. The children have their own Kids' Story Time every Saturday.

Young readers (ages twelve-young adult) are also at home in their room on the second floor. Working closely with the McKinney Independent School District, McAndrews carries the required readings. Special events, such as a Harry Potter release party, attracted more than 800 guests.

Nonfiction, historical fiction and romance titles are on the third floor. Four original jail cells from the 1880s are still on the third floor with comfortable, cushioned bunks to sit and browse. The cells house historical fiction, Texas history, American history and world history sections.

McAndrews is also available to host your special meetings and events. Your guests will have access to all three floors of the exquisitely renovated historic building. The highly skilled culinary staff can customize a menu perfectly suited for your event and budget. The buffet-style menus make for a simple yet elegant occasion. Special items such as cakes and pastries are also available. They can customize a beverage selection suitable to the food menu including coffee drinks, cold drinks, wines and liqueurs.

McAndrews Bookshop and Café supports the community through programs that donate books to church libraries, host private book clubs, and house community meetings, networking groups and business breakfasts. They are proud members of the McKinney Chamber of Commerce, Better Business Bureau, and McKinney Main Street.

The word is spreading about this unique bookshop. Customers travel from all around Collin County, Garland, Fort Worth, Melissa, Allen, and Plano to enjoy the atmosphere and books at McAndrews. McAndrews Bookshop and Café is a family place owned by a great family.

For more information, please visit or call 972-547-9555.

Dallas Area Rapid Transit

Dallas Area Rapid Transit (DART) moves more than 200,000 passengers per day across a 700-square-mile service area that includes Dallas and twelve surrounding cities.

To promote ridesharing, DART also operates a system of high occupancy vehicle (HOV) lanes used by more than one hundred thousand commuters each weekday.

As a regional transit agency, DART is funded with a one-cent local sales tax. The service area consists of thirteen cities: Addison, Carrollton, Cockrell Hill, Dallas, Farmers Branch, Garland, Glenn Heights, Highland Park, Irving, Plano, Richardson, Rowlett, and University Park.

DART began operations January 1, 1984, and the board and staff worked quickly to plan bus service improvements, rail transit, HOV lanes, carpooling services, and transit for the mobility impaired.

DART is headquartered at 1401 Pacific Avenue in downtown Dallas. With about 3,000 employees and contractors, the agency serves the area with approximately 130 bus routes, 45 miles of light rail transit, 31 freeway miles of HOV lanes, and paratransit service for the mobility impaired. DART and the Fort Worth Transportation Authority (the T) jointly operate thirty-five miles of commuter rail transit (the TRE), linking downtown Dallas and Fort Worth with stops in the mid-cities and DFW International Airport.

DART also drives development throughout its system. Through 2005, $3.3 billion in private funds was invested in developments along DART's forty-five-mile light rail system serving Dallas, Garland, Richardson, and Plano. Between 1997 and 2001, office properties near suburban DART Rail stations increased in value fifty-three percent more than comparable properties not served by rail.

From downtown Plano to downtown Dallas and beyond, DART is driving developers to create innovative "transit villages" that provide a new live-work-play lifestyle and reduce the need for private vehicle trips. Economists at the University of North Texas conclude that, "Clearly, DART is helping to stimulate the local economy and bring new vitality to the City of Dallas and the core areas of DART's suburban member cities."

One of those leading the way in smart growth is Richard Howe, the developer behind Fifteenth Street Village, a four-building complex with townhouses and condominiums near DART's Downtown Plano station. "The transit village is a great example of the new urbanism, and DART is obviously an integral part of that," says Howe.

Robert Shaw, who built Eastside Village and a second rental community near the Downtown Plano Station, said, "I think everyone now generally recognizes that building near transit is a big positive. It's like waterfront property—it's physically limited and can't be duplicated just anywhere."

Through 2014, the DART Rail System is slated to double in size to ninety-three miles. Extensions now in development include the 17.5-mile Northwest Corridor serving Downtown Dallas, American Airlines Center, the Dallas Medical/Market Center, Love Field Airport, and the cities of Farmers Branch and Carrollton. A fourteen-mile branch will extend from the Northwest Corridor to North Irving's Las Colinas Urban Center and DFW International Airport. Another 10.2-mile extension will serve the Southeast Corridor connecting Downtown Dallas, Deep Ellum, Fair Park, South Dallas, and Pleasant Grove. In addition, service will extend south three miles from Ledbetter Station in South Oak Cliff to I-20 and northeast five miles from Downtown Garland Station to Rowlett.

For routes, schedules, maps and other information, visit DART's website at www.dart.org.

SALINAS CONCRETE L.P.

For nearly three decades, Salinas Concrete L.P. has specialized in residential concrete, slabs, driveways, patios, walkways and light excavation. It all began in Houston in 1982 when Osiel Salinas founded the company after coming to the United States in April of 1979 and working with his cousin, Antonio Molina, Sr., from whom he learned everything about residential concrete construction. In 1985, Osiel relocated the business to Plano and operated for many years from his own residence. In 2003, Salinas Concrete moved to its current location at 6817 K Avenue, Suite 103 in Plano, Texas.

Osiel married Claudia in 1992 and they have four daughters—Dennice, Karina, Cecilia, and Clarisa. Salinas Concrete is such a family business that their youngest daughter, Clarisa, often advises that perhaps her folks should get another job because they talk about the work so much when they are at home. However, she is always quick to add that she would be willing to help at the office, as she gets older so she will be in charge in the future.

Osiel attributes the company's continued growth and success to his father, who taught him to work hard and to always be honest and fair. With a total of eighteen full time employees, Salinas Concrete is proud to join nationally recognized builders such as D.R. Horton, which is listed in the NYSE, Kimball Hill Homes, Standard Pacific Homes, MRL Construction, Sterling Designs and other custom builders in construction projects across the region. The company has grown from starting 700 homes in 2002 to over 2,200 homes in 2004 and 2005 in the Dallas/Fort Worth area.

Salinas Concrete also operates in Baton Rouge, Louisiana. Salinas Concrete is a member in good standing of the Home Builders Association, the Plano Chamber of Commerce and the U.S. Chamber of Commerce. The company also sponsors local baseball and soccer teams.

With over $25 million in sales two years in a row Salinas Concrete has established itself as a very reliable company eager to take on new challenges.

In the future, the Salinas family looks forward to expanding the company into other cities, as well as completing a building for their own company in the form of offices on two acres in East Plano.

Salinas Concrete L.P. can be reached at 972-509-8184.

Above: Osiel Salinas founded Salinas Concrete in April 1986.

Below: Osiel and Claudia Salinas.

Allison & Johnson, LLP

Family Law

Strategies to solutions...problem-solving...trial skills...collaborative and resourceful. Each of these phrases characterizes the essence of business at Allison and Johnson, LLP, a full-service family law practice devoted to helping clients across North Texas. The firm was recognized for excellent competence and ethics in 2005 and 2006 by being named to the "2005 and 2006 Bar Register of Preeminent Lawyers" by Lexis-Nexis® and Martindale-Hubbell®.

Kip Allison was named a 2006 "Texas Super Lawyer," and Jody Johnson was named a 2004-2006 "Texas Super Lawyer" and and 2005-2006 "Top 50 Women Lawyers in Texas." Associate Barrett Stern was named to the 2007 "Texas Rising Stars" list.

Kip Allison and Jody Johnson formed Allison & Johnson in 2001.

In 2001, Kip Allison and Jody Johnson combined twenty-six years of legal experience to form a partnership just two weeks before tragedy struck the nation on September 11, 2001. It was a difficult time to venture into such a major business commitment, but their dream of opening a boutique family law firm that would exceptionally serve the residents of Collin County and its surrounding communities as finally becoming a reality.

Located inside the Legacy Bank Building in Plano, today Allison & Johnson, LLP, is a moderate size law firm that includes four attorneys and four administrative staff members. Dedicated to providing the highest quality in legal services and expertise, caseloads are limited, as clients have come to admire and expect the firm's unique and personal attention to detail. Additionally, the firm utilizes state-of-the-art technology and a team approach to maximize the outcome of a case. Talented professionals such as accountants, financial planners, appraisers, and mental health professionals are recruited to address all aspects of a client's case and to prepare clients "to move forward in their next phase of life."

The firm employs a broad range of services to family law clients that relate to issues of divorce, custody and visitation, child support, post-divorce modification, enforcement, paternity, family violence, mediation, and the unique process of collaborative law—a process that is client-centered and avoids court intervention.

The hallmark of Allison and Johnson, LLP, is providing comprehensive and realistic advice to clients to create opportunities for settlement whenever possible, and thorough preparation for trial success when necessary. The firm uses traditional litigation methods along with alternative resolution methods such as collaborative law to achieve client goals and communicates with clients to problem-solve issues and ensure that well-informed decisions can be made. The firm understands that each family matter is the client's, not the firm's, and that the decisions made may significantly impact children and other extended family members.

Allison & Johnson, LLP, is a member of the Plano Chamber of Commerce, and three of the four attorneys reside in Collin County. All four attorneys are active in their churches and other extracurricular activities with their families. For more information about Allison & Johnson, LLP, please call 972-608-4300 or visit www.aj-familylaw.com.

Barry Benton Photography, Inc.

Barry Benton believes that classic photography belongs in the realm of fine art. And every time he picks up his camera, he proves it.

One of the most experienced portrait specialists in the Southwest, Benton is a respected photographer with a state-of-the-art photography studio. His photographs represent precious moments in time that last forever when captured by his camera.

A photographer since 1980, Benton specializes in capturing the people and places of Texas, especially those in Collin County. Located in Plano, He specializes in family, wedding, and commercial photography. He holds many honors including "Best Photographer in Collin County" from 2003 to 2005 in a reader's choice survey by Star Community Newspapers, and "Official Photographer of '21 for the 21st Century.'" *Collin County Kids* selected Benton as "favorite photographer" in its inaugural "Family Favorites" survey.

"I provide both my commercial and family clients with distinctive images they are proud to display or pass down from generation to generation," Benton said. "My location and nature images focus on the area's personality and provide a visual walk through the beauty of life, especially that within Collin County."

Photography service companies tend to lean toward one of two distinct personalities. Some are driven from an art perspective and others are more business oriented. The more successful organizations are able to balance art and business qualities. Benton's background in photography and business enable him to mix the two aspects and operate a successful photography business.

Benton's photography experience began in high school working on the high school newspaper and yearbook photography staff. He spent a summer working for his local newspaper doing darkroom work and photography.

Benton graduated from Louisiana Tech University in 1987 with a B.S. in business administration with a marketing option. While attending college he was on the yearbook and college newspaper photography staff doing photography and darkroom work. In 1986, Benton began managing the local Party Pics franchise in Ruston, Louisiana, specializing in event photography on and near campus. Barry managed part-time photographers, scheduling, bookkeeping, marketing, operations, and customer management.

Since 1987, his career has involved sales and account management. Benton's experience in sales enables him to effectively understand his customers' objectives and provide them with a product that meets those objectives.

Benton took a hiatus from photography, working in the sales side of a software company in Houston. "Following a downturn in business following the tragic events of September 11, I was laid off. At that time, I decided it was time to get back into photography and opened Barry Benton Photography, Inc." he said.

Barry Benton Photography provides romantic storytelling wedding photography that combines the best of contemporary and traditional approaches. Services include storytelling and traditional approaches to photography utilizing color and black and white images to capture the special moments of the day.

BBPI offers Collections (packages) and ala carte options for clients. "Our approach is to offer a basic coverage that will be the minimum that we will contract for," he said. "From that base, we will work with clients to build an appropriate Collection, which may consist of additional coverage hours and proofs, large print album, parent's album, thank you notes, prepaid enlargements, rehearsal dinner coverage, etc."

With corporate photography, BBPI has built a customer base among small and medium businesses in the Collin County and Dallas area by focusing on special events, such as Christmas parties, as well as corporate events such as seminars and conventions.

With family photography, Benton strives to achieve uncommon results by working with families to understand their expectations, wants, and environment. BBPI makes every effort to provide a creative and lasting portrait that the family will enjoy for many years. As a customer service-oriented company, it strives to make it easy for clients to recommend its service to their friends, colleagues, and families.

Benton hopes to continue providing outstanding customer service, professionally artistic photography, and smart business.

For more information about Barry Benton Photography, please call 972-758-1051 or visit www.bentonphotography.com.

DFA, Ltd.

DFA, Ltd. is a Family Limited Partnership formed in 1989 as an investment holding company for the family of Don Day. The company has three areas of focus. Its first area is purchasing and renovating commercial historic buildings for long term investment. DFA has renovated eighteen historic buildings in McKinney, and twice received the city's annual award for Best Preservation of a Commercial Historic Building.

The company's second area of business is the development and construction of quality office buildings.

The final area of business is the development of retail businesses, restaurants and a hotel in downtown McKinney.

The shareholders of DFA are Don Day, Craig Day, Lisa Day and Dana Day Micinski. Craig supervises all construction projects and Lisa directs the accounting and management of outside investments while managing her own separate retail pet accessory store. Dana is a member of the family committee that sets policy for new investments and company directions.

Don is general partner of DFA and oversees all project planning, land acquisition, financing and design. He is a graduate of the University of North Texas with a physics degree and has over forty years of experience as developer/contractor on more than one hundred properties including historic renovations, high rise office buildings, medical office buildings, hospital additions, apartments and shopping centers in ten states.

Don is also a past member of the City of McKinney's Housing Authority, Transportation Committee and Bond Election Board. He was founder and chairman of the McKinney Citizens for Economic Growth, the PAC that spearheaded the drive to legalize the sale of beer and wine in McKinney.

He is currently active on several community boards including: chairman of Tapestry Healthcare Development Inc, a Community Clinic that provides medical services to the more than fifteen thousand residents of McKinney who are uninsured or do not otherwise have access to healthcare; vice-chair of the City of McKinney's Planning and Zoning Commission; a Main Street Board member, a McKinney Housing Opportunities Board member and president of the McKinney Downtown Property Owners Association.

DFA, LTD has had two basic philosophies throughout its existence; to insure long term security for the company and the Day family; and to make a contribution back to the local community to make it a better place for all those who live there.

✧

Above: Don Day.

Collin County Hispanic Chamber of Commerce

In 1998 a countywide Chamber of Commerce was formed and incorporated in the State of Texas to inform and inspire the Hispanic business community. The Collin County Hispanic Chamber of Commerce (CCHCC) focuses on empowerment of all minority populations interested in business issues. Three community business-owners came to the realization that there was no organization dedicated to the improvement of business for Hispanics in Collin County. They were Delia Lujan, merchant in McKinney; Pedro Peña, photographer in Wylie; and Humberto B. Rodriguez, property investor in Melissa. As the first officers and directors, they determined the policies of the chamber that still govern decision-making: fairness, equality, and leadership opportunity.

The CCHCC has become more widely recognized during the past five years of civic and commercial activity in the county; it is now counting its members in the hundreds.

Growth of the membership in CCHCC reflects the increase of Hispanics in business and in the general population of Collin County since 2000. The Hispanic Chamber is a forum of information for entrepreneurs, small business, and established companies; the information may be obtained in English or Spanish. CCHCC provides activities that enrich and expand the members' lives, not only in business but also in education and culture. CCHCC also enjoys participation with other chambers in Collin County and the other Hispanic chambers of North Texas through business seminars, expositions and mixers.

The chamber's membership is comprised of individuals, companies and organizations that are Hispanics and "Hispanic friendly;" and the goal is to provide access to companies and organizations committed to working with our community. The group estimated that by 2005, Hispanics represented about a third of the county population, in line with national averages. At the same time, Hispanic businesses represent only about 15 to 20 percent of the businesses in the area. As the community grows, businesses all interested in tapping this market will also grow. The chamber's objective is to continue growing and solidify its function as the main point of contact for any group or organization that wants to access the Hispanic businesses and professionals of Collin County.

In August 2005, CCHCC organized and sponsored the first Hispanic Business Expo of Collin County named Viva Collin County! The expo is open to individuals free of charge and features dozens of vendors interested in offering its products and services to Hispanic consumers and businesses. CCHCC plans to continue organizing this expo every year and grow it into a powerful celebration of Hispanic culture in Collin County.

The chamber offers a wide range of services to each of its members, including the promotion of member's businesses; business referrals and leads; business expos; monthly meetings and monthly luncheons; breakfast networking; after-hours networking; access to community and business calendars of activities; member discounts; access to the chamber's official newsletter, *CONEXIONES*; access to one-to-one consultation and training through SBA programs; special offers negotiated for Chamber members with different publications in North Texas; InterChamber networking activities and joint programs with Hispanic and non-Hispanic chambers in North Texas; and joint programs and networking activities with the Hispanic Business Alliance (HBA).

The 2005 Board of Directors includes Rodney E. Cruz, chair; Rick Troutman, vice-chair; Monica Alvarez, secretary; Humberto B. Rodriguez and Rafael Gutierrez, directors. 2005 Officers on the Executive Committee are: Arturo Ibarra, executive director; Tres Garza, executive director-elect 2006; Carol Rodriguez, secretary and treasurer; Jose Castro-Frenzel, Membership; Estella Prettelin, communications; Walter Unglaub, community relations; and David Trujillo, youth relations.

For more information visit the CCHCC website at www.cchchamber.org.

Above: (From left to right) Chairman of the Board Rodney E. Cruz; Founder Humberto B. Rodriguez; Vice-Chair Rick Troutman; Not pictured are Secretary to the Board Monica Alvarez; and newly elected 2006 members Engineer Manny Molera; and Attorney Donald H. Flanary, Jr. and restaurateur Arduro Ibarra.

Below: (From left to right) Membership Director Jose Castro-Frenzel; Chamber Officer in 2005 Walter Unglaub; Chamber Officer in 2005 Carol Udel-Rodriguez; Executive Director 2006 Tres Garza. Not pictured are Youth Activities Director David Trujillo; and newly elected 2006 members Executive Director Elect Francisco Ibarra; Secretary Contessa Seabolt; Treasurer Barbara Oldenburg; Communications Estella Prettelin; Member Services Ricardo "Rick" Ortiz; and Community Relations Luis Crespo.

CENTENNIAL MEDICAL CENTER

✧

Above: Labor and Delivery at Centennial Medical Center.

Below: Centennial Medical Center.

An exceptional standard of quality healthcare debuted in June 2004 as Centennial Medical Center opened its doors to residents of Frisco and the surrounding communities. The center offers a broad range of services including advanced technologies for convenient, secure electronic access to patient information; GE digital imaging for all radiology services, including mammography; women's services, including nine labor-and-delivery rooms, a 32 bed nursery, 14 bed neonatal intensive care unit (including Level III), 40 private beds for post partum and gynecological services, and two caesarean section suites; an interventional heart program that includes cardiovascular surgery; surgical suites utilizing minimally invasive technology supported by full clinical information systems; a 21-bed emergency department; and critical care and medical/surgical services.

Centennial Medical Center is located on a forty-acre campus and is the first acute care hospital in Frisco, employing over 500 people, 600 medical staff personnel, and offering 118 licensed beds with a future capacity of up to 190. Residents from Frisco, North Plano, McKinney, Allen, Prosper, Celina, Anna, Princeton, Blue Ridge, Melissa, Wylie, Little Elm, and The Colony and surrounding areas can all take advantage of the hospital's exceptional care and successful

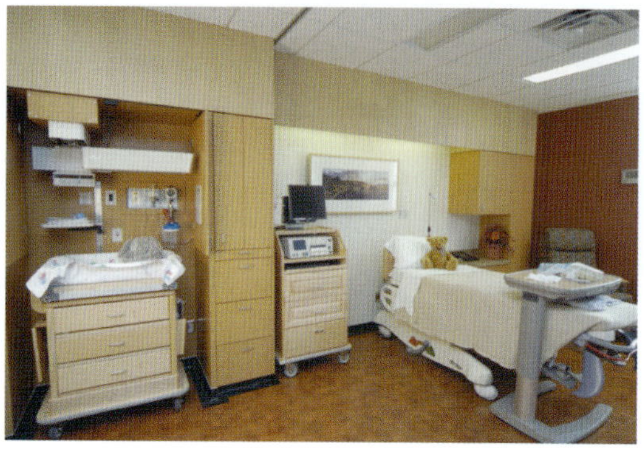

outreach programs including community health fairs and educational events.

As Centennial continues to provide advanced medical technology and service-oriented programs, plans are being made to offer urgent care and imaging services in the community, improving accessibility and convenience for customers—right where they live.

Honored to be Frisco's only full service hospital, Centennial Medical Center is a member of Tenet Healthcare Corporation's extensive family of medical facilities located around the country, and emphasizes its key mission as a provider of quality healthcare services that are responsive to the needs of the community.

Centennial Medical Center, through the Tenet Healthcare Foundation, supports local charitable and community-supporting organizations and activities. Scholarships for education are provided through grants benefiting the Frisco Independent School District (FISD) Matching Donor Program and the Collin County Community College Foundation, and through Centennial and the Tenet Healthcare Foundation's participation as a sustaining partner of the FISD Education Foundation. The Foundation's support of the Frisco Family Services Center, Leadership Frisco's recently implemented Children's Clinic for uninsured children and Children and Community Health Center-McKinney provides additional assistance and care to many of the needy in Frisco and Collin County. Local support is also provided to the Arthritis Foundation, American Heart Association, American Cancer Society, American Diabetes Association, and C. H. Hale Prostate Cancer Foundation.

Mexi-Go Restaurant

Mexi-Go Restaurant is a company that focuses on the upscale-casual segment of the food market, serving authentic Mexican cuisine as well as fresh Tex-Mex in a casual setting.

Jose Jaimes and his wife, Paula, opened the first Mexi-Go location on November 15, 1990, in North Dallas. Jaimes was first introduced to the restaurant industry in 1985 as he held a position at Chuck's Hamburgers. After working for the company for six years, he saw an opportunity when a yogurt shop next to Chuck's went up for sale. He reached an agreement and decided to open as a three man, six-table operation.

The timing was right, as the Mexican food industry was one of the fastest growing areas of the restaurant market to this day. Defying the odds as an economic recession settled in, the company continued to grow so fast that it became profitable after just six months.

In the beginning, the restaurant was so small that when large groups would come to dine, patrons would be crowded into tables arranged to allow for maximum seating, which often left many people sitting near the door or by the restrooms. Even when the restaurant moved to a larger location it was still madness. The cashier could not keep up with people trying to pay and the lines only got longer.

During the bonanza of the 1990s, Mexi-Go opened its second location in Allen, Texas, on October 13, 1998. The store became an immediate success until it was rocked by an uncontrolled growth spurt of restaurants in the area. During this time, many restaurants came and went, but Mexi-Go stayed due to its loyal and strong customer base. In 1999 the company welcomed the addition of Mexi-Go Delivery located in a growing area of North Plano. In September 2003 a West Plano location was opened, taking the Mexi-Go brand name to the next level and fulfilling a growth strategy. Mexi-Go has averaged a new store opening every five years and offers a full array of banquet and catering services for corporate and private events.

Over a decade later, the company remains most proud of its roots as a family-owned business that grew from nothing and without any outside investment. Mexi-Go currently employs eighty hardworking people generating sales of over $3.1 million with locations in Plano, Dallas and Allen. Always looking for new opportunities to expand, Mexi-Go is planning store openings across Texas, Arkansas, Missouri, Georgia, and Tennessee.

Mexi-Go is committed to the local economies of the cities in which they operate, bringing jobs and tax revenue. The company also participates with local charitable organizations and provides donations and discounts for school organizations.

Mexi-Go is headquartered in Allen at 533 West McDermott and may be accessed online at www.mexigo.com.

Owner Jose Jaimes.

GenerationNext Telecommunications, Inc.

In the ever changing, fast-paced world of telecommunications, Michelle Lenker and the employees of GenerationNext Telecommunications, Inc. (GXT) have developed a company unmatched in expertise and experience in the field today. Providing the highest quality and most cost effective alternatives to creating, maintaining or complimenting in-house engineering, construction, installation, and project management organizations, GXT tailors its service to the needs of every customer.

Though today the company is involved in a number of multimillion-dollar projects and includes a team of engineers, project managers, CAD technicians, and support staff members, GXT's continued success was originally built upon the independent spirit and sheer determination of its founder and president, Michelle Lenker.

In 2001, Lenker entered a new phase in her twenty-four-year career in telecommunications after leaving her former employer, MCI. With over two decades of experience in the field, she knew the telecom industry well and believed that this was her opportunity to create her own company.

Financial support was nearly impossible to find, as banks were unwilling to fund such a venture in the volatile telecom market at the time. She remembers the experience well, "I had seven doors slammed in my face. Banks would not even talk to me."

Lenker realized that the only way to accomplish her goal was to use her own money. Three years later, with the grace of God and the unwavering support of her right arm, Jo Ann Parkinson, and husband, Roger, she received a loan through a small business development program and GXT successfully found its place as "the leading edge in a high tech world."

Today, the company is involved in everything from feasibility studies and engineering, to field surveying, permitting, and construction management. AT&T, MCI, Qwest Communications, WilTel, and SBC are just a few of the leading clients who have outsourced the design, construction and engineering of their networks to GXT.

From packaged to turnkey solutions, GXT has dedicated itself to offering the best and most qualified services available in the market today. Project managers oversee the construction and delivery of an entire program from start to finish, while in-house telecom professionals offer proven consulting services that keep projects successfully on track. Telecommunications staff members are available for the full- or part-time needs of customers and GXT prides itself in being able to deliver a total project team to oversee issues that can arise during any given situation.

GenerationNext Telecommunications, Inc., (GXT) is located at 850 Central Parkway East in Plano. For more information, please visit www.gxtltd.com.

Medical Center of Plano

Since opening in 1975, Medical Center of Plano has provided Plano and Collin County with superior healthcare. They've built their reputation on the exceptional compassion they offer to every patient—a genuine legacy that has been preserved from the group's simple beginning as a small community hospital. Now a full-service, state-of-the-art facility offering the latest in technologies and a comprehensive range of healthcare services, Medical Center of Plano continues its growth to maintain its position as a leader in healthcare.

Medical Center of Plano includes a 427-bed acute-care facility with more than 1,500 employees and over 1,000 staff physicians, representing more than 70 specialties and subspecialties. The fifty-three-acre campus includes the main hospital and medical offices, an outpatient surgery center, a comprehensive cancer treatment center, an emergency center, a radiology/imaging center, complete maternal and child health services including a high-risk antepartum unit, a neonatal intensive-care unit, a comprehensive cardiovascular program, and The Center for Lifestyle Enhancement.

The medical staff at Medical Center of Plano is a diverse group of outstanding professionals dedicated to using new technologies and remaining up-to-date on current advancements in healthcare. Nurses, radiologists, therapists, pharmacists, support staff, management and administration are focused on the health and comfort of every patient who comes through the doors. Caring for the whole family, as they would their own, is what the men and women of Medical Center of Plano do best.

Medical Center of Plano is a vital part of the community through the creation of jobs, payment of taxes, and giving back with time, talent, and dollars. Employees support numerous nonprofit agencies through their volunteer efforts, while health seminars, wellness programs, and free screenings are more popular than ever. Attendance at support group meetings continues to grow as this foundational spirit of caring and community pride infuses every area of Medical Center of Plano.

Approved by the Joint Commission on Accreditation of Healthcare Organizations, Medical Center of Plano was named one of the nation's "100 Top Hospitals" in 1998. The recipient of several healthcare-excellence awards over the years, it was also named "Best Hospital" and "Best Emergency Room" for the ninth year in a row in *Star Community Newspaper*'s 2005 Reader's Choice Awards.

Medical Center of Plano is located at 3901 West Fifteenth Street in Plano and on the web at wwwwmedicalcenterofplano.com.

✧

Above: Medical Center of Plano in 2005.

Below: Medical Center of Plano in 1975.

Ann & Nate Levine Academy

A Solomon Schechter School

Above: At Levine Academy the five-to-one student teacher ratio builds strong bonds between students and teachers.

Below: Ann & Nate Levine Academy is located at 18011 Hillcrest Road in Dallas.

Ann & Nate Levine Academy, a Solomon Schechter School, is a Conservative Jewish day school that has offered outstanding education in a Jewish environment since the academy was founded in 1979. Previously known as Solomon Schechter Academy, the Levine Academy is one of the leading academic institutions in the Dallas/Fort Worth area and is open to students of any race, color and national or ethnic origin who are being raised within the traditions of normative Judaism. Classes are offered from preschool through eighth grade.

Providing our students with a well-rounded education also means teaching them to become caring and compassionate people who will make a difference in tomorrow's world. In preparing our students for such a journey, our school and all of its teachings rest on a solid foundation of Inspiration, Knowledge and Character.

- Inspiration: At the heart of Levine Academy's success is our award-winning faculty. Our five-to-one student-to-teacher ratio builds strong bonds between teacher and student, which encourages and supports our students toward academic excellence and social success.
- Knowledge: Our secular and Judaic curriculum challenges our students to maximize their academic potential resulting in more than mastery of content. They develop tools for self-learning, analytic thinking and the courage to question and probe in their search for the truth. Our graduates are well prepared to succeed in high school and beyond.
- Character: In our family-like atmosphere, students from diverse ethnicities and backgrounds, bond as a community of creative, responsible, and caring individuals. Our Ethical Covenant provides the core values that are central to our school's philosophy–responsibility, respect, justice, citizenship, caring, holiness and integrity. These are traits we hope become an integral part of our students' character.

Other unique aspects of a Levine Academy education include:

- An average class size of fifteen students, plus the expertise of a resource team, ensures that students receive the individual attention and guidance they deserve.
- A faculty, averaging nineteen years teaching experience, committed to the total education of its students.
- A curriculum that takes the students outside the classroom for field trips and on major educational retreats throughout the year to such destinations as historic Texas, Washington, D.C., New York and Israel.
- Extracurricular activities play an important role in shaping a child's mind and we offer a variety of activities including numerous after-school clubs. Middle school students can also participate in the National Junior Honor Society, Student Congress, or serve as Student Ambassadors.
- In addition to an exceptional educational program, Levine Academy offers an award-winning sports program, music and drama, computer skills, and a multi-faceted art program.
- To help students achieve their full academic potential, we offer Individual Learning Plans for sixth and seventh graders, (which will be expanded to all grades within the coming years), as well as our newly introduced Challenge and Discovery Program, a school-wide project designed to provide for the individual learning styles, interests and abilities of each student.

Ann & Nate Levine Academy is located at 18011 Hillcrest Road in Dallas, Texas and for additional information on the Ann & Nate Levine Academy, visit the website at www.levineacademy.org.

Dallas Stars Hockey Club

Dallas hockey has come a long way since its first team, the Texans, hit the ice in the fall of 1941. At the time, it was advertised as "the most dangerous game in the world…with playing speed, flashing blades, and crashing bodies."

Nearly seven decades later, the region's premier hockey club offers the very best in sports entertainment, both in product and value. The Dallas Stars Hockey Club is a professional hockey club and member of the National Hockey League (NHL) and was originally founded as the Minnesota North Stars in 1967. In the winter of 1992-1993, owner Norm Green picked Dallas, Texas, as the new home for the club. The group played its first season in North Texas in 1993-1994, with home games at Reunion Arena.

Just as the Dallas Stars Hockey Club was making its Texas debut, Michigan native Jim Lites was welcomed as the group's first president. Lites, who had served as executive vice president of the famed Detroit Red Wings for eleven years, was faced with "growing the sport of hockey" in a nontraditional market like Texas and graciously accepted the new challenge. With the help of Green, who served as the club's owner until he sold the team to Tom Hicks in 1996; Bob Gainey, the team's head coach in the first couple of seasons and general manager of the club; Jeff Cogan, Lites' right hand man in marketing hockey in a sunbelt city and chief marketing officer, now president of the Texas Rangers; and Rick McLaughlin and Bill Strong, hockey was back in "Big D" with a vengeance.

Though the region's history had included hockey for some time, the sport had not yet become the amazing success, with its large fan base and sold-out games, when the Dallas Stars debuted in the '90s. At the time, there were no high school hockey teams in the Metroplex, six sheets of ice, and only about 250 kids playing ice hockey in and around the city. Today, there are 64 high school hockey teams, 30 sheets of ice, and 5,500 kids playing the game.

These numbers can be attributed to the unfailing vision and dedication of Lites. He insisted that the Stars invest in ice rinks and sell the sport to families. Thus, the Dr Pepper StarCenters were born and now include eight complexes in Dallas/Fort Worth. The team sold the sport as "football on ice," with hard-hitting action that was fast and full of energy.

Teaching the main rules of the sport proved to be a challenge, but the key marketing tool was simply trying to get people to sample the product in person. Many fans admit that they were "hooked" after they went to their first hockey game in person.

Today, the club continues to play a vital role in the area through its Dallas Stars Foundation. Founded in 1996, it serves as a positive force throughout the Dallas/Fort Worth Metroplex and is focused upon providing support to children of the community so they may lead quality lives. Through teamwork, interaction, and education, the Dallas Stars Foundation works to bring together all members of the Metroplex and build a bright future for everyone.

Today, the Dallas Stars Hockey Club is headquartered in Frisco at the Dr Pepper StarCenter at 2601 Avenue of the Stars and includes nearly ninety full-time employees. Game highlights and extensive information about the team and its players is also located on the Internet at www.dallasstars.com.

Above: The Stars and Mike Modano have been facing-off in Dallas against the best in the NHL since 1993.

Below: The Stars won the Stanley Cup as champions of the National Hockey League in 1999.

Cooper Aerobics Center

Founded in 1970 by Kenneth H. Cooper, M.D., M.P.H., Cooper Aerobics Center is known as a leader in the wellness and preventive medicine field. Cooper Clinic, a preventive medicine facility that provides a comprehensive examination for identifying significant preventable threats to one's health, was opened first along with the Cooper Institute, a nonprofit research and education center dedicated to looking at the relationship between physical activity and overall health. Since the beginning, all Cooper Aerobics Center programs have been medically supervised and based on proven science.

Cooper Aerobics Center has grown from the original two entities to eight on its thirty-acre campus in north Dallas. In addition to the Clinic and Institute, it includes an award-winning fitness center, a one- or two-week behavior modification program, a multivitamin and nutritional supplement line, fitness and wellness consulting, and a hotel and day spa.

The original location is joined by the first-ever expansion, Cooper Aerobics Center at Craig Ranch in McKinney. The new facility includes a seventy-five-thousand-square-foot fitness center and a day spa, with a Cooper Clinic preventive medicine facility planned for late spring 2007.

Like the Fitness Center on Preston Road, Cooper Aerobics Center at Craig Ranch membership includes a medical component—a treadmill stress test, body composition analysis, and blood lipid profile from Cooper Clinic. Initiation to the center also includes a fitness evaluation and a tailored exercise program based on those results. A private fitness consultation, one-hour personal training session and nutrition education helps members get off to the right start in their fitness journey.

In addition to the enthusiastic and well supervised kick-off, each new member receives innovative on-going programming which helps to keep Cooper members and residents of the Craig Ranch community motivated and in-the-know about lifestyle enhancement.

The facility houses top-of-the-line exercise amenities including a large training area, the latest in cardiovascular and resistance training equipment, Olympic-sized pool, full Cardio Theater, an indoor and outdoor track, tennis courts, sand volleyball, indoor basketball court, a climbing wall, and several group exercise studios.

The overall feel of Cooper Aerobics Center at Craig Ranch provides the ideal balance between high energy and relaxation. Cooper Spa at Craig Ranch offers the perfect getaway for members or the public. Like its counterpart, Cooper Spa on Preston Road, the day spa at Craig Ranch offers a wide array of services including massages, facials, exfoliating scrubs, body wraps, pedicures, and manicures.

Cooper Aerobics Center is located at 12200 Preston Road in Dallas and Cooper Aerobics Center at Craig Ranch is located at 7910 Collin McKinney Parkway in McKinney. Both locations can be reached via the web at www.cooperaerobics.com.

Above: Dr. Kenneth H. Cooper.

Below: Guests receive expert advice as they begin a personalized fitness program at the Center.

Plano Tire Company, Inc.

Since opening in March 1973, Plano Tire Company, Inc. has provided quality auto service and retail tire products with efficiency, integrity, and commitment to every customer. Built on what once was the site of a tractor repair shop located at 1516 North Central Expressway, Plano Tire Company, Inc. was originally created in addition to Dallas Wholesale Tire, a company owned by Bob Griffin and managed by Gene Sparks.

Plano Tire Company, Inc.'s three founders, Bob Griffin, James Sparks and Gene Sparks, opened their store with four employees and six operational bays. Originally, the shop took care of tires, front-end alignments, and brake service, but today is a full-service auto repair shop, successfully competing with many of the large discount organizations in the area.

Today, Gene Sparks is the company's sole owner after purchasing his partner's stock interests. Gene's wife, Doris, serves the company by working in the office and taking care of the finances. Although not employed by the company, Gene and Doris' daughter Amy was born the same month the company was started. Their son, Bill, grew up in the business and now owns and operates his own business in Phoenix, Arizona.

Between 14 and 18 employees work for the company today and revenues continue to reflect a successful locally owned, independent dealer, while maintaining a strong advantage over their competitors. This advantage is due to a strong community commitment, flexibility, and a desire to grow right along with the needs of the local community.

One of Plano Tire Company's goals is to provide a good, rewarding and secure working environment for their employees. Long-standing employees include Jerry Bennett, who has driven the service truck for 23 years, and Frank Chick, the company's front-end specialist for 20 years. Other employees pictured above have been with the company for two to fifteen years.

Today the company is proud to serve a wide customer base that includes commercial, retail, municipalities, utility companies, construction, government entities, and national accounts. Roadside service, not common to tire companies today, is still offered by Plano Tire. A future goal is to expand the company's line of performance products while retaining loyal customers and meeting new ones.

Giving back to the community has always played an important role at Plano Tire Company as they have supported and continue to support area schools and churches, PTA organizations, the Junior League of Plano, Collin County Children's Advocacy Center, United Way Board for Collin County, Substance Abuse Prevention Agency of Plano, YMCA, and Chamber of Commerce.

Plano Tire is affiliated with local, state, and national organizations supporting the tire and auto industry. Gene has served in leadership positions and strives to support his customers with knowledge of current products and technology.

For quality tires, expert service, or friendly, free advice call 972-423-5545 or browse the company's website at www.planotire.com.

Above: Back row (from left to right): Mike McCann, manager, Jose Funes, Gary Bardin, Frank Chick, Jerry Bennett, Luis Frias, and James Barrett. Front row (from left to right): Rachel Hill, Doris Sparks, Gene Sparks, and Doug Carder.

Below: Gene and Doris Sparks.

Marshall V. Johnson, D.D.S., M.S., P.A.

Dr. Marshall V. Johnson, DDS, MS.

Since 1989, the office of Marshall V. Johnson, D.D.S., M.S., P.A., has devoted itself to the dental practice of periodontics and implantology. After completing his residency in periodontics in 1989 from the University of Missouri - Kansas City, founder Marshall Johnson knew Plano was the perfect home for his budding practice.

Today, he is driven by a mission to offer his patients the premier periodontal practice in North Texas by delivering quality care and customer service to the best of his abilities, supporting and creating an environment for doctors and staff to grow in skill, knowledge and financial success, and building and enhancing relationships with other offices and patients. Dr. Johnson and his staff strive to deliver more than their patients and referring offices expect in an individually tailored manner.

When Marshall opened the practice, he spent a lot of time on the road. He was becoming acquainted with the dentists and orthodontists in neighboring cities, and he worked at building a reputation that would ensure these new acquaintances would feel comfortable in referring their own patients to him.

Over a decade later, the goal of the offices of Marshall V. Johnson, D.D.S., M.S. remains to provide patients with the highest quality care in a compassionate and safe environment. In order to ensure this type of atmosphere, the most current periodontal procedures, instruments, medications, and sterilization techniques have been implemented.

Whether patients need basic periodontal treatment, such as dental implant placement, crown lengthening, bone grafting, antibiotic treatment, or ridge augmentation, Dr. Johnson and his staff are ready and able to assist. Each procedure is done with the patient's comfort and safety in mind. The office also works closely with the patient's general dentist to ensure that the patient gets the best possible result in accordance with their wishes.

Dr. Johnson was a serious student and received a number of awards during his education including: the Distinguished Student Award from Texas A&M, Dean's List at Baylor College of Dentistry and Chancellor's Award from the University of Missouri-Periodontics. He is a firm believer that a true professional must remain state-of-the-art and takes over fifty hours of continuing education each year. Much of this advanced education is in Implant Dentistry, Bone Regeneration and Cosmetic Procedures. Dr. Johnson is also one of the few periodontists that have gone on to achieve the status of Board Certified Diplomate in Periodontics.

Dr. Johnson is a member of all relevant professional societies, including American and Texas Dental Associations, Greater Plano, Dallas and Fourth District Dental Societies, American Academy of Periodontology, and Southwest and Texas Societies of Periodontists. He is also involved in the community and serves on the boards of directors of Leadership Plano and the Plano YMCA, serving for fifteen years on staff at the Medical Center of Plano, coaching youth baseball, basketball, and soccer, and as a member of the Plano Rotary Club.

For more information about Marshall V. Johnson, D.D.S., M.S. visit www.jjperio.com.

Arts of Collin County

In 2004, city officials and community leaders in Collin County founded the Arts of Collin County Commission, Inc., in response to the interest expressed from citizens for a world-class arts center.

To ensure all citizens can share and enjoy the full diversity and vitality of the arts, the Arts of Collin County will, in its first phase, build a center with a 2,100-seat multipurpose theatre and multiple spaces to showcase the visual arts. This complex will serve as an anchor for a planned arts district.

Through a cooperative effort between the three cities of Plano, Allen, and Frisco, $57 million in public bond monies have been designated to build the arts facility. Private funding will be secured by the Arts of Collin County Foundation, Inc., to supplement the funds received from the public sector.

When completed, the new facility and arts park will not only provide a venue for quality arts and entertainment; it will improve the quality of life and education of county citizens. Thirty-plus organizations will provide over 250 performances each year for more than a half-million patrons in the performance and outdoor venues. Special events for end of year holidays, the Fourth of July and other times will be provided on the site. Facilities will be available to both commercial and nonprofit organizations for events.

The generosity of several leaders in Collin County has propelled the fundraising efforts through the donation of the 124-acre site near State Highway 121 and Custer Road, valued at over $22 million by Briar Ridge Investments; and a $1-million pledge from Kathryn and Craig Hall of Hall Financial Group.

Dr. Robbie Robinson and Dr. Betty Muns of Plano, Mayor Pro Tem Maher Maso, and Nick Barretta of Frisco, and David Sterling of Allen comprise the Arts of Collin County Commission as its founding leadership board. James Baudoin is executive director and also serves as project manager.

The stellar design team for the project includes BOORA Architects of Portland, Kirkegaard Acoustics of Chicago, park landscape planning by Hargreaves Associates of San Francisco, and Theatre Projects Consultants of Norwalk, Connecticut. Hunt Construction Group serves as contractor.

Groundbreaking for the first phase is scheduled for 2007 and a thirty-month construction schedule is anticipated. The core elements included in the first phase are: a twenty-one-hundred-seat multipurpose main theater, a lobby with a café and gift shop, a sculpture garden and art terrace, an art gallery, a community performance room, edu-cation facilities, an outdoor event meadow and concert stage, and hike and bike trails. In this phase thirty-two acres are set aside as open space, creating a "Central Park" for Collin County.

For more information about the exciting future of the Arts of Collin County, visit www.artsofcollincounty.org or call (214) 495-5800.

Above: An artist's rendering of the view of Performance Hall from the meadow.

Below: An interior view of Performance Hall.

Legacy Heart Center

Legacy Heart Center's medical complex at 6601 Preston Road in Plano is billed as Collin County's most comprehensive collection of outpatient cardiac diagnostic testing and treatment services under one roof.

The center, which opened on April 18, 2005, covers 43,000 square feet of office and laboratory space in Legacy Park and is home to Legacy's 15 cardiologists and more than 100 other medical and administrative staff.

The mission of Legacy Heart Center is "to exceed the expectations of our patients and our referring physicians by providing the best possible cardiovascular care in a caring and responsive environment." said Waenard Miller, M.D., F.A.C.C., and Legacy's managing partner.

With the prevention of heart attacks and strokes as a key focus, Legacy Heart Center has added a LightSpeed computed tomography (CT) system to its array of leading-edge cardiac diagnostic testing and treatment services, becoming the first private cardiology practice in North Texas with the advanced CT scanner.

The LightSpeed scanner allows Legacy Heart Center cardiologists to non-invasively capture exceptional high-resolution images of vascular structures, the heart and coronary arteries in less than ten seconds. This allows cardiologists to complete a thorough, non-invasive cardiac exam that detects any blockages in the coronary arteries and provides a coronary calcium score that can be used to assess future heart disease risk.

Dr. Miller said, "These efforts are all part of trying to prevent heart attacks and strokes. This technology is really on the leading edge of being able to detect what we call "pre-clinical" disease, meaning there is a disease process going on but it has not yet reached the degree at which it may cause symptoms, much less a stroke or a heart attack. We can do something to make a significant difference in a person's life if we catch these problems early."

What does the future hold? According to Dr. Miller, "Now that we have the ability to more easily look for pre-clinical disease, we want to become a resource and help make a difference in the lives of our Collin County neighbors. Since there is a large number of young people here who deal with a lot of high stress jobs and pressures that can increase cardiac problems, we really want to become a resource for area companies, to help get their employee base healthier. We know we make a difference because we've got proven treatment options and medications."

Legacy physicians also treat patients at the primary medical centers in Collin County, including Baylor Regional Medical Center at Plano, Presbyterian Hospital of Plano, Medical Center of Plano and Medical Center of McKinney.

For more information on Legacy Heart Center, please visit www.legacyheartcenter.com or call the center at 469-326-3400.

MobileComm Professionals, Inc.

MobileComm Professionals, Inc., a wireless engineering services company, specializes in the Design and optimization of the cellular networks. Their services results in seamless wireless network coverage with strong signal providing conventional voice and third generation data services.

MobileComm's commitment to provide cost-effective solutions to the wireless industry, without compromising quality, has resulted in rapid growth for the company. Since its beginning in 2002, the company has seen record annual growth of over hundred percent every year.

Before founding MobileComm, current CEO Harvinder Cheema, President Gurmeet Likhari and Vice President Jacob Idichandy were managers for Marconi, a British telecom products and wireless consulting services firm. When the company began restructuring, the three decided to organize their own business. Although they faced numerous challenges and had little operating cash, they chose to self-fund the company's needs. From the beginning, MobileComm's focus has remained clear—to focus on wireless design and optimization.

MobileComm employs the most skilled telecom engineers, forming a team of highly talented professionals

Cheema, Likhari, and Idichandy believe the key to the company's success is maintaining the highest quality standards. The company is ISO 9001 certified, the highest quality accreditation a company may earn. Another factor in the firm's success is providing these services in the most cost effective way.

MobileComm has received Tech Titan Award two years in the row, ranking fourth in 2004 and first in 2005 in the "Fastest Growing Category," organized by the Metroplex Technology Business Council.

In addition MobileComm ranked seventeenth in the professional services category, and ninth in the South West region, in the *News India-Times*/VII-100 List of privately held, Indian-owned companies in America.

MobileComm, headquartered in Plano, has more than a hundred employees with engineers located in most major cities, including Boston, Chicago, Houston, Atlanta, Spokane, San Francisco, Los Angeles, Seattle, Denver, and Kansas City.

MobileComm regularly reaches out to local schools to help develop the skills needed for this highly technical field. The company hires local college graduates and technicians from technical institute. The company's philosophy is to provide opportunities for those with enthusiasm and an aptitude to learn.

The future is very bright for MobileComm, its employees and clients. Mobile applications and Information technology services for small and medium businesses are on the horizon, giving the company an opportunity to work with non-telecom businesses. Services and products ranging from web application development, networking solution, and customized software will help businesses increase their efficiency. And if that helps to increase the world productivity and profitability, which is just what the founders of MobileComm Professionals would want.

For more information on MobileComm Professionals, Inc. visit www.mcpsinc.com.

✧

Top: Harvinder Cheema.

Middle: Gurmeet Likhari.

Bottom: Jacob Idichandy.

Plano Chamber of Commerce

Since 1946, the Plano Chamber of Commerce has provided educational programs, networking opportunities and advocacy on the local and state level for the Plano business community.

When a small group of businessmen joined forces to create the Chamber, it was formally incorporated as a nonprofit with forty members. The city's population at the time was a mere two thousand.

The Chamber played a vital role in creating a strong infrastructure in Plano. In the early 1950s, members lobbied the Texas legislature for creation of the North Texas Municipal Water District. Members also took a leading role in extension of the North Central Expressway.

During the 1960s, the Chamber became the leading business and social entity in the community. Popular skits during the annual banquet were written, directed, and performed by Chamber members and attracted capacity crowds.

Ground was broken at the Chamber's current location at 1200 East Fifteenth Street in 1974 and the staff moved into the new facility in 1975.

Plano's population had soared to thirty-four thousand by the mid-1970s, creating a boom in retail business. To balance this rapid growth, the Chamber formed a team to seek out new industry to compliment the two major firms—Georgia Pacific and Stewart Manufacturing—that had already moved to Plano. By 1979, Plano had won twenty-three new industrial prospects and more than a hundred businesses valued at $9.3 million now called Plano home.

By the mid-1980s, membership in the Plano Chamber had topped 1,200 members and the organization continued to be instrumental in area economic development efforts. The Plano Economic Development Board was formed in the late '80s and took over those responsibilities, but the two organizations still work closely together and have positions on each other's Boards of Directors.

The Plano Chamber began focusing on smaller business owners in the 1990s with networking and educational programs designed to help owners grow their businesses. The '90s also saw Plano named an All-America City.

As part of the Chamber's fiftieth anniversary celebration in 1996, ground was broken for a new Chamber building addition.

Today, the Plano Chamber of Commerce operates with a staff of nine employees and serves a membership of more than 1,500. A large group of ambassadors and volunteers donate their time to aid staff members in the coordination of key divisions.

The Plano Chamber produces numerous publications for its members and the community, including an Annual Membership Directory, Business Plan/Annual Report, Newcomer's Report, Clubs & Organization's Directory, and Plano Area Map.

For additional information about the Plano Chamber of Commerce, visit its website at www.planochamber.org or call 972-424-7547.

SPONSORS

For more information about the following publications or about publishing your own book, please call Historical Publishing Network at 800-749-9790 or visit www.lammertinc.com.

Black Gold: The Story of Texas Oil & Gas

Historic Abilene: An Illustrated History

Historic Amarillo: An Illustrated History

Historic Anchorage: An Illustrated History

Historic Austin: An Illustrated History

Historic Baton Rouge: An Illustrated History

Historic Beaufort County: An Illustrated History

Historic Beaumont: An Illustrated History

Historic Bexar County: An Illustrated History

Historic Brazoria County: An Illustrated History

Historic Charlotte:
An Illustrated History of Charlotte and Mecklenburg County

Historic Cheyenne: A History of the Magic City

Historic Comal County: An Illustrated History

Historic Corpus Christi: An Illustrated History

Historic Denton County: An Illustrated History

Historic Edmond: An Illustrated History

Historic El Paso: An Illustrated History

Historic Erie County: An Illustrated History

Historic Fairbanks: An Illustrated History

Historic Gainesville & Hall County: An Illustrated History

Historic Gregg County: An Illustrated History

Historic Hampton Roads: Where America Began

Historic Henry County: An Illustrated History

Historic Houston: An Illustrated History

Historic Illinois: An Illustrated History

Historic Kern County:
An Illustrated History of Bakersfield and Kern County

Historic Laredo:
An Illustrated History of Laredo & Webb County

Historic Louisiana: An Illustrated History

Historic Midland: An Illustrated History

Historic Montgomery County:
An Illustrated History of Montgomery County, Texas

Historic Oklahoma: An Illustrated History

Historic Oklahoma County: An Illustrated History

Historic Omaha:
An Illustrated History of Omaha and Douglas County

Historic Pasadena: An Illustrated History

Historic Passaic County: An Illustrated History

Historic Philadelphia: An Illustrated History

Historic Prescott:
An Illustrated History of Prescott & Yavapai County

Historic Richardson: An Illustrated History

Historic Rio Grande Valley: An Illustrated History

Historic Scottsdale: A Life from the Land

Historic Shreveport-Bossier:
An Illustrated History of Shreveport & Bossier City

Historic South Carolina: An Illustrated History

Historic Smith County: An Illustrated History

Historic Texas: An Illustrated History

Historic Victoria: An Illustrated History

Historic Tulsa: An Illustrated History

Historic Williamson County: An Illustrated History

Iron, Wood & Water: An Illustrated History of Lake Oswego

Miami's Historic Neighborhoods: A History of Community

Old Orange County Courthouse: A Centennial History

Plano: An Illustrated Chronicle

The New Frontier:
A Contemporary History of Fort Worth & Tarrant County

The San Gabriel Valley: A 21st Century Portrait